NOV 108

Child
Of
The Land

Available from Artscript
Publications in North America.
Trafford Publishers in the UK.

www.childoftheland.ca

Written compilation and layout: Doug Greenfield.
Editor and advisor: Maggie Greenfield.

Additional writings by Doug & Maggie Greenfield displayed at:
www.artscriptpublications.ca

Contact the author: tech@artscriptpublications.ca

Order this book online at www.trafford.com/07-2073
or email orders@trafford.com

Most Trafford titles are also available at major online book retailers.

Note for Librarians: A cataloguing record for this book is available from Library
and Archives Canada at www.collectionscanada.ca/amicus/index-e.html

Printed in Victoria, BC, Canada.

ISBN: 978-1-4251-4810-2

*We at Trafford believe that it is the responsibility of us all, as both individuals
and corporations, to make choices that are environmentally and socially sound.
You, in turn, are supporting this responsible conduct each time you purchase a
Trafford book, or make use of our publishing services. To find out how you are
helping, please visit www.trafford.com/responsiblepublishing.html*

*Our mission is to efficiently provide the world's finest, most comprehensive
book publishing service, enabling every author to experience success.
To find out how to publish your book, your way, and have it available
worldwide, visit us online at www.trafford.com/10510*

 www.trafford.com

North America & international
toll-free: 1 888 232 4444 (USA & Canada)
phone: 250 383 6864 ♦ fax: 250 383 6804 ♦ email: info@trafford.com

The United Kingdom & Europe
phone: +44 (0)1865 722 113 ♦ local rate: 0845 230 9601
facsimile: +44 (0)1865 722 868 ♦ email: info.uk@trafford.com

10 9 8 7 6 5 4 3 2

Forward

Child of The Land is a true story written as a record of my childhood growing up on a homestead in northern Alberta. It is also a story of how the experience of that simple, wholesome beginning gave me a vital foundation on which to build an exciting and adventurous life to come.

Furthermore, it is written to commemorate my parents. I am deeply thankful for all that I learned from them as they laboured to raise their children and develop our family business.

The names in this book have not been changed to protect the innocent because, as I recall, none of us were very innocent! We were all full of fun, mischief and tomfoolery. We saddled every adventure that rode by and gave our parents good reason to grow old.

Dedication

"Child of the Land" is dedicated to my four wonderful daughters, **Kerri**, **Bonnie**, **Debbie** and **Julie** whom I will always love immeasurably.

In this book, you will find that each chapter embraces a different topic that sequentially recounts the experiences of that theme from my childhood beginnings to fruition in adult life. Each is a story of how every aspect of homestead life had an impact upon my future years and that almost all that I needed to know about life, I learned from the land.

Child
Of
The land

An autobiography by
Douglas Warren Greenfield

Contents

Peace Country Pioneers
A poem commemorating the many
contributions of The Peace River Country
Pioneers

There's a land where the forest was endless
As wild as anyone knew,
With skies that push back the horizon
And sparkle a crystalline blue.

This land is all but exotic
With profusion of colour and sound,
A place alive with such beauty
It's known the whole world around.

This is the land of great rivers
The Wapiti, Smoky and Peace,
Whose waters all flow to the Arctic
And into the ocean release.

It's here men desired to settle
To call the wild lands their own,
It's here I was born on the homestead
And it's here that will always be home.

Child of the Land

Our parents were young and so hardy
They came to begin a new life,
It was vision and love that empowered them
In this land of struggle and strife.

They hacked and they dug and they laboured,
Our folks changed the face of the bush
From a forest of aspens and spruce wood
To farmland so fertile and lush.

Those pioneers now are retired
They fought the good fight and they won,
And left the land open and useful
For the next generation to come.

With these humble lines I commend them,
Contributions they've made to the land
Will ever be seen and remembered,
While we their children still stand.

We stand in this life as they taught us
Strong with resolve from the start,
And forever we are the thankful
For their gift of a pioneer's heart.

Douglas W. Greenfield

Acknowledgments

The historical details in this book are drawn for the most part from my memory, fifty odd years after the fact. Therefore, I want to thank those friends who have helped to refresh the memories of my childhood and most formative years.

Thank you to:

My best Friend, who lives in high places, without whom, life as I enjoy it would be meaningless;

Maggie Greenfield, my faithful, darling wife and best friend for her patience, perseverance and unmatched love. For her valuable input and tireless editing of my feeble attempt at this writing;

Francis Willard Greenfield, my father, whom I must thank for so much of my basic and valuable education, who, with eyes closed, becomes a storyteller extraordinaire, remembering life as it was so many years ago;

Mrs. Peggy Ulland (Gartly), our friend who experienced life on the homestead as mother, wife, businesswoman and teacher, whom I appreciate for her keen intelligence and sharp memory;

Mr. Bruce Grant, our friend who also challenged the northern life with family and business, and succeeded, and whose children reflect his influence in stewardship and business;

Mrs. Anne Donaldson, our friend, author and chronicler of life on the homestead, who has written several valuable books of her own about life in the north of Alberta.

Mrs. Dolly Barnhardt for her influence and contribution of good memories upon my life these many years. You will always be "Mom" to me.

Thank you also to our many proofreaders for your keen eyes and good suggestions.

Preface

At sea with my heart in the land

"Burst, Burst, this is Captain Kidd, radio check, over..." The ship's radio broke the early morning silence. At that moment, the intercom blasted, "This is the Executive Officer speaking. Prepare for heavy weather ... I repeat ... prepare for heavy weather!" When the intercom went silent, I returned my call to the H.M.C.S Mackenzie. "Captain Kidd, this is Burst; you are loud and clear, over." "Roger, Burst, Captain Kidd out," came the reply. We were one of three Canadian destroyers preparing to join a large Commonwealth naval exercise in the South Seas and were travelling to join the fleet in Sydney, Australia.

The sea became increasingly rougher as the morning went on. The forecast we received from the Wellington weather office yesterday as we left harbour had not been promising, and now the ship's company was busy preparing for hurricane force winds.

Later that night, lying asleep, I was dreaming of my home in northern Canada, when the duty Radar Plotter shook me awake at midnight. "Greenfield," he whispered, "you're on watch again." I rolled over and tried to forget where I was, remnants of sweet dreams still floating through my consciousness. For just a moment, I lingered back on the old farm, savouring the luscious aroma of sweet clover as the dream faded into the present. My bunk heaved hard to port and then a moment of near weightlessness came while the ship plummeted over a huge wave. I timed my descent from the top bunk with the heaving of the ship, being careful not to awaken my sleeping shipmates. The familiar whine of the ship's main turbines was now accompanied by a symphony of creaking and moaning sounds caused by heavy seas.

When my ship slammed into the trough of yet another monstrous wave, steel moaned and the ship shuddered under the strain. As we surfaced out of that wave, I quickly clambered down from my bunk, staggering under the extra g-forces created by the ship's now powerful upward thrust. Boot lockers were banging in and out from under the bunks while clothing swung restlessly from hooks overhead. Once dressed, I fought my way down the ladder from my sleeping quarters and headed to the galley, hoping to find something nourishing to eat before going on watch. Moments later, I came away with a delectable ketchup sandwich and headed for the Operations Room.

Stumbling down Burma Road, the ship's main passageway, with one foot on the deck and one on the starboard bulkhead, I realized that we were quartering a very heavy sea. This was going be a rough watch to stand. The Operations Officer was on duty when I arrived at my station in the Operations Room. "How's your stomach, Greenfield?" he winced through clenched teeth. "Oh, I'm all right," I told him, licking the ketchup off my lips. "I never get seasick." He peered over the plotting table at me with a look of envy. "I hope you're right. You're going to need it tonight," he said as he clung to the overhead wireways for balance. I then scrambled up the dark passageway to the bridge, noticing that the lookouts were huddled inside and there were scarce few men in sight. Fighting to keep my balance, I stood at a forty-five degree angle holding onto the window ledge and looked out at the dark sea. Through the blackness, one could just make out the forward three-inch-seventy gun with its huge barrels turned back toward the bridge and lashed down to the deck with heavy hurricane straps.

We surged over the top of a gigantic wave and crashed down into the next black trough, sending sea water right over the bridge and onto the quarterdeck. The duty Watch Officer handed the Coxswain a slip of paper, "Secure all upper deck hatches and pass the word. The upper deck is out of bounds until further notice." "Yes sir," the Coxswain said as he headed down the hatch.

"Twelve zero zero," I wrote in my log. "Day two, crossing the Tasman Sea in rough weather. No contacts on radar at this time except the Mackenzie, our consort, two miles off the port beam." By 02:00 the wind was steady off the port quarter. I was secured to my radar console by a length of nylon rope that helped to relieve some of the heavy, physical strain caused by the ship's constant movement. The door opened from the bridge above just as the ship heaved abruptly to port, sending the Watch Officer crashing through the opening and into the bulkhead at the bottom of the ladder. "Are you alright, Sir?" I called, trying to untie myself from the console. "Ugghh," he moaned, as he crawled to my radar indicator and hauled himself up off the deck. His hat was askew and he looked very tired. "Your ear is bleeding a little," I offered, as he regained his balance. Without speaking, he donned the head set from above the plotting table, and using the ship's radio call signs, he transmitted a squadron directive, "Captain Kidd, Captain Kidd, this is Burst, over." "Captain Kidd," came the reply. "Just passing on the latest weather," he called. "Winds from the south-southeast at sixty-eight nautical miles per hour, wave action is seventy feet even. Make sure your upper deck is out of bounds and your lookouts remain inside. Burst, out."

Then, pausing a moment and noticing me clinging to my radar PPI, he asked, "Are you OK?" "Oh sure," I said, "this doesn't bother me. What I don't like is the smell of vomit from down below." "Yeah," he said, "the smell doesn't help, does it? I need to get someone outta the sack to clean Burma Road. There is so much slippery puke in the corridor that it is dangerous to walk." With that, he left the Ops Room and disappeared down the hatch looking for some poor boatswain to attend to cleanup detail.

As the night wore on, my ribs became tender and bruised from slamming into the machinery, and my arms tired from hanging on. The radar was so cluttered from gigantic waves that a real contact likely wouldn't show up in all this mess anyway. My job was

12

to watch for other shipping but the only friendly contact out there was the IFF return off of the Mackenzie two miles to my port side.

Two hours later, I keyed the intercom. "Bridge, Ops, I am leaving the Operations Room to wake my relief." "Roger, Ops," they called back. After rousing Werner and warning him to wear his shoes when he went up, I went back to resume my duties. The smell was a little better after someone had cleaned the main passageway, but the washrooms were still bad and the galley was completely shut down. Now I wished I'd hidden food in my locker instead of that 'forty' of rum. What was it that my Chief Petty Officer always told me? Oh yes, "A complaining sailor is a happy sailor." Right!

Twenty minutes later, Werner dragged himself up the companionway and leaned against the doorway, looking tired and sick. The St. Croix gave a mighty shudder as she buried herself into the trough of a monster wave and then strained to raise herself out from under the tons of foaming sea water again. "Did you sleep?" I asked my relief, as he braced himself between the radar indicator and the plotting table. "Not a lot," he said, yawning. "What's going on up here?" "The Mackenzie is still our consort two miles to port," I told him. "The wave action is now almost eighty feet from crest to trough with the wind speed at seventy knots. There is so much sea clutter on the radar that I can't tune it out, so all you can see is our consort once in a while. The Watch Officer has posted the upper deck out of bounds, and you, my friend, are going to have a delightful dogwatch! Did you get something to eat?" "Nope," he mumbled, "the galley is closed and there were only crackers left before I crawled into bed. Not even any coffee." "Well, it'll be dawn soon," I told him, "and the cooks will be up. As for now, all you can see outside is the phosphorescence in the water. Otherwise, it's totally black." Werner tied himself to the radar and I headed for the hatch and anxiously back to my pillow and my dreams.

Within minutes, my deep weariness erased all consciousness of the ship's movement, as memories of Canada's northland once again filled my dreams. Reality drifted away and I found myself balancing tenaciously on a slippery log, midstream over the creek. Patches of snow still lingered in the shade of the trees and large pieces of ice floated by in the swift water. Halfway across, now, I fought for my balance, affected by the movement of the stream below. In one moment of terror, my foot slipped off and dropped me hard on my chest against the log. Flailing wildly, I was drawn backward into the rush of cold, spring water. Frightened and freezing, I was being swept away in the black, rushing water of Fox Creek.

Hazard or humour, it is all the same in the end

Only six years old and far from the protective care of my parents, one learns quickly that the only way to survive is to struggle, fight and never give up! The wild lands of the great Peace River Country were, for me, a garden out of which grew knowledge, skill and adventure, preparing me for the future. From hard work and family fun to wild encounters with danger, life was never dull. Adventure began the moment I was old enough to walk and was experienced daily through resident wildlife, comical neighbours and crazy experiments. Hazard or humour, it is all the same in the end. Once you are safely home again, the incident becomes a memory to be shared and the daily experiences of life are told and retold for others to enjoy.

Most often, one thinks of a *pioneer* as an elderly person who has experienced life the way it was in the very early years of our country's development. This is, of course, entirely true, although they were *young* at the time. My parents were among the early settlers in the area. Their achievements are remarkable, and we are indebted to them for granting us the opportunity of sharing in their joys and struggles and for teaching us much of what we would need to know to succeed in this crazy world.

I was born in that exciting and adventurous time when the great "Peace River Country" in northern Alberta was being developed, and so, experienced the beauty and peace of the land in the course of everyday life on the homestead.

I sometimes think that if the Veteran settlers in our area had been remotely aware of all the work and difficulties they would face, they might have abandoned the whole plan and moved east, not west!

Most of this vast, forested area had suffered a great fire years earlier but was now covered with a thick blanket of new tree growth, which meant that the young men and women moving into the area had to transform the bush into farmland before they could even begin.

They knew, of course, that they would have to break the land and make do for a season until that first precious harvest was in. But, I sincerely doubt that they could have anticipated the knee-deep mud, the monster mosquitoes or those inevitable long and cold winters. Nor could they have predicted just how many years of backbreaking effort would be required to prepare the land, remove the stumps, pick and burn roots, plant crops and gardens and raise a family. All the while, they milked cows and fed pigs and chickens at the beginning and end of each tiring day.

Then after the chores were done and the firewood was brought in, there was time to relax by the fire and rest their weary backs. This was a time to reflect and be thankful for the many good things that the Peace Country had to offer, including skies so big and blue, there was barely room for the horizon. There were starlit nights so bright that you could easily see where you were walking, and air so sweet it seemed to nourish you with each breath. Life, for me in the northland, was incredibly vibrant and full of wonderful expectation!

I vividly remember the quiet evenings, our little home awash with lantern light. Mom would knit or mend while Dad talked of the day and their dreams for the future. We would sit close to the oil stove as Mom read a bedtime story, or Mom and I would cuddle under a blanket, enjoying homemade music as Dad played his violin.

Hard times seem to draw people together and cause us to focus our minds on the simple things of life that are so good. Our contentment did not depend on our monetary investments, but on less tangible things such as love and commitment, faith and trust, honesty and integrity. These were the simple pleasures of life that helped to sustain us, like the ever-present support from neighbours and friends, warm milk fresh from the cow, new potatoes or wild strawberries. Whether we had bright, winter days or busy, warm summers, a spring full of new life, or crisp, colourful autumns, these uncomplicated joys established in me a standard for my life today. Those were rich days in my childhood, when I knew little else but this incredible land and the love and warmth of my home and family.

We were living examples of the fact that although life can sometimes be hard, it can at the same time, be enjoyable and present valuable experiences and good memories. It was in this era, which in contrast, seems so far from life today, that I lived and grew as one of the "Little Pioneers of the Peace River Country."

Chapter
One

Great anticipation

The Greenfield Family History

My family's heritage began in Canada near the turn of the century. In 1905, my grandfather, Ewart Greenfield emigrated from Manchester, England and married a lovely lady from North Dakota named Etta Ferguson. Together, they claimed a homestead near Long Lake in the fertile farmland of central Saskatchewan and settled in to build a life and a family.

By 1918, World War One had just been won and Canada was recovering from a great loss of men and resources. The following year, as the Northwest Mounted Police were being re-formed into the Royal Canadian Mounted Police service, my father and mother were born on their Saskatchewan farms.

During those years, most farmers still worked the land with horse-drawn equipment, and most houses did not have indoor plumbing. Newspapers and crystal radio receivers were the only available forms of media, and live musicians played at virtually every dance. Most country schools consisted of only one room, housing a gamut of children from grade one to high school (often only to grade eight). The one-room schoolhouses of that era were heated by a central, wood or coal stove, and often had their own stable. School bathrooms were outhouses located out in the fresh air, sometimes attached to the stables. Some of the more fortunate children rode to school on horseback, but because this was an economically depressed era, most students came to school on foot. Since there was little cash for hiring workers, many of the older children stayed

20

home during the spring seeding season and each fall at harvest time to help on the farm.

By today's standards, life in those days appeared to be much harder, but no one complained, because at the time, this was considered normal. In fact, my grandfather went to work in the dusty fields each day, wearing a jacket and tie! (Talk about dressing for success!) The history of Gibbs and Govan, Saskatchewan where my parents were raised has been eloquently recounted in several books described by the pioneers of their generation.

By September 1939, Britain was forced to declare war against the advancing Nazi regime in Germany, and our Prime Minister, William Lyon Mackenzie-King declared war soon after. With our country still recovering from the loss of 60,000 men during World War One, everyone was hoping for a time of peace. Sadly, peace would have to wait as we were now drawn into yet a second world war. By the spring of 1940, out of duty for his country, my father joined the Canadian military. Initially in the Army, he trained at Dundern, Saskatchewan but transferred at the first opportunity to the Royal Canadian Air Force. Dad completed his training at St. Thomas, Ontario and joined the 161st Squadron on the east coast. He served as an aero engineer flying a Canso submarine chaser throughout the war years from his station at Torbay, Newfoundland.

RCAF 161 Squadron's flying boat, the Canso.

During W.W.II the Royal Canadian Air Force, Eastern Air Command, employed the use of Canso PBY 5A, amphibians to protect Canada's east coast and provide air support to Naval convoys crossing the Atlantic. The Canso was powered by two 1200 HP Pratt & Whitney Wasp engines, had a wing span of 104 ft. and an effective patrol range of over 2500 miles.

Frank Greenfield, an engineer, shown here in the gun blister of the Canso

In July of 1942, while on short leave from the squadron, Mother and Dad were married back in Saskatchewan, thus beginning a solid lifetime commitment to marriage.

Frank and Marjorie married July 25, 1942

My grandmothers and grandfathers continued the struggle on their prairie farms while their children were off at war. My mother's family, the Hamptons, became one of the many to grieve the loss of a child overseas. Their second eldest son, Bill Hampton, a pilot officer, was shot down and killed behind enemy lines. Those were days of meagre hope, looming fear and constant tension as the world was again at war.

I mention these early days of lean existence and hard times in order to accurately depict the troubled era that our parents had just endured. After five long years, the war was finally over, and people again looked forward to building a new and prosperous life.

Venturing north to the Promised Land

In 1945, when my father's tour of duty was complete, my parents moved to Edmonton, where they worked to save up some money. They had heard that the Government of Alberta was making farmland available to veterans, so in the spring of 1946 they bravely ventured north to the Peace River Country.

This was indeed a time of great anticipation! A world war had just been won, and mankind, for the moment, seemed to be free of impending evil. From the onset of the Great Depression until the winning of World War Two, Canadians had known little more than fleeting hope and hardship. This had been an era of scant prosperity, and the whole country suffered because of it. The war had employed most of the young men and women in their prime, those who would be the next generation of business owners and homemakers. Canada's slim coffers had been used to fund the war effort rather than build essential roads and facilities needed to develop the Canadian northwest. Now, thousands of war veterans were streaming back home from their stations across Canada and overseas, full of excitement, hoping to build a new life.

In those years, the narrow dirt road from Edmonton northward meandered through miles of untamed forest, across the river at Athabasca and through the bogs along Lesser Slave Lake. Despite the remoteness of the land and what might seem to be discouraging circumstances along the way, they were sustained by their hopes and dreams. The economy was growing and there were great opportunities just waiting to be discovered in the North.

Dad had purchased a 1928 Dodge sedan in Calgary when he left military service. This handy vehicle had now become their moving truck, loaded down and heading north. Their Winnipeg couch was roped across the front bumper and two large trunks were tied on the back bumper with all their worldly possessions crammed inside.

Upon reaching High Prairie, the gateway to the "Land of the Mighty Peace," the dense forest opens up into rich land, suitable for farming. Here, my parents dreamed of building a fine life in a new and exciting land. It was this great anticipation that fuelled the fire of hope in every early pioneer as they came to begin a new life.

The Peace River country is characterized by an immense span of rich, forested land, brutally divided by deep, river channels. It was some of this rugged land that was made available to surviving veterans as homestead land.

Moving North in the '28 Dodge

Those big rivers, though scenic to behold, became vast obstacles to ill-equipped settlers pushing their way into this Promised Land. The other great barrier was the sheer expanse of unrelenting bush! The thousands

27

of hectares of aspens, birch, spruce and willow covering the land were, if nothing else, an indication of the wealth of the soil. Unfortunately, the expense of removing that bush to claim the land for agriculture was most often beyond the means of early settlers, so the Alberta government embarked upon a *project* to clear the land and render it accessible to the homesteaders.

One man was chosen to undertake this task, and his name was O.B. Lassiter. Mr. Lassiter, already in his seventies, would soon command a small army of men and machines to tackle the enormous task of clearing 100,000 acres of bush land for agricultural use.

Arriving in the Peace Country at that time in history was opportune, in that there was much work for those with youth and vision. Sawmills were turning out needed lumber for the building boom in the area, and thousands of acres of land were being cleared for farming. The Alaska Highway was still under construction and every hopeful community along the railroad was expanding.

My mom and dad initially set up their tent in a muddy field in the *metropolis* of Spirit River near today's main street. Soon, they found work in the picturesque Blueberry Mountain area nearby. Here again, they erected their tent, this time near the sawmill that operated where Moonshine Lake Provincial Park is now.

Living on love

That first winter was, I am sure, a cold one for my parents, living in a 12 ft. by 12 ft. canvas tent on the frozen ground and going to work each day at the sawmill. Let no one tell you that people cannot live on love and determination alone, because my parents did and flourished.

The following winter, wanting to move up in the world a little, they moved into a small building which had been my Uncle Bob's chicken house, only a couple of miles from the mill.

The next year, they moved again, this time east to the hamlet of Wanham, and again erected their tent home. Here, the bustling Lassiter clearing camp was established, with its large crews of 'Cat skinners' and support staff, daily stripping the land of unwanted forest.

My dad, a trained aero engineer, went to work that year operating a D8 Caterpillar tractor (Cat). These were good days in my parents' youth, hard but fun, as they made new friends and shared the pioneering spirit with so many others. Dad worked 12-hour shifts on that belching old Cat, claiming the land for future farmers, while mother worked long hours at a local restaurant.

They eventually purchased a little 12 ft. by 20 ft. cabin from one of Lassiter's crewmen. That one thousand dollar purchase was only a shack, but was to become home-sweet-home for many years to come.

The word *Project* in those days was of course an expression that referred to the Lassiter clearing project. It was this rugged area that would eventually become home to many a pioneering family. If ever there was a government make-work project, this was it! The Cats had been reclaimed from the Alaska Highway development and some from as far off as the Aleutian Islands. The maintenance and operations were manned with every available, unemployed hopeful that could be found. Thus, the land was cleared and the great Peace Country farming block took shape.

By the spring of 1949, Lassiter had cleared as far north as the hamlet of Eaglesham, some twenty miles to the east of Wanham. By that point he had completed almost one hundred half-section homesteads, cleared of the bush and available for settlers. Each half-section is 320 acres, and enough to begin a small farming endeavour for those tenacious dreamers and would-be homesteaders.

A cross-cultural experience

The little community of Eaglesham was reportedly named after a village in Scotland by the same title. It was a small, rail-side village, comprised mostly of farming settlers from across the country, and in fact from around the world. The buzzword across the nation at that time was "The Peace River Country." This was toted as the land of opportunity for all, the mosquitoes not mentioned! Indeed, many people came to see.

Year by year, newcomers arrived full of expectancy of what they might find in this highly acclaimed land, people of diverse nationality and culture from war-torn Europe to the Canadian north. Dutch, German, Ukrainian, Polish, Swedish, Scottish, Irish, English, French and a few Native Indians, to name some, were the men and women who settled and developed *our* Peace River Country. In time, such distinctively different and interesting people as these became our neighbours and our friends. A grand cross-cultural experience such as this presented a rare educational element that would positively shape my attitude and my worldview as I was growing up.

The summer of '49 was very busy, as my folks had relocated from Wanham to the community of Eaglesham in order to stay near the clearing project. The pungent smell of brush-burning smoke lingered across the land, and the community teemed with working men and women.

Laughter on the project

Dad was one of the many operators running Cat that spring, cutting trees, routing out stumps and piling the brush ready for burning. More than once, a Cat operator would tree a black bear and signal another Cat-skinner to come and push the tree over. This newly found sport helped to pass the weeks of monotony those men had to endure. Of course, being young and agile, I don't suppose they ever considered the danger an angry, wild black bear might actually present.

Cat operators also had to continually invent new ideas to keep awake during long shifts in the bush. The great danger would be that an unnoticed tree trunk might slide up over the cutter or through the brush piler and crush the operator in the cab of the Cat. Occasionally, one Cat would run up on the back of another with the operator sound asleep, a tactic that was sure to waken a man out of the sweetest dream. Since the government had yet to construct roads in the area, the workmen would often have to navigate back to base camp at night by the stars. It was prudent to learn which star was *actually* the North Star, and periodically, someone did fail to show up at shift end because of a navigational error.

Father tells the story of his friend Rex, who, while cutting brush, routed a sleepy black bear from his den. Rex, not wanting to be attacked by the disgruntled creature, attempted to crush it with the heavy steel cutter on the front of his Cat, but to his frustration the clever animal managed to elude him. Time and again, he lifted the cutter, repositioned the Cat and slammed it down again, hoping to kill the bear.

Dad was operating nearby, watching Rex's futile antics with amusement. Finally, Father signalled for Rex to lift his cutter as high as he could, then reposition the Cat, first this way, then that, and then slam the cutter down. Rex watched anxiously over the side of the noisy Cat as he slowly raised the equipment up again, but the crafty bear was nowhere in sight. Suddenly, Rex gave a yell and was seen bailing headlong over the back of his running machine! The frightened animal had become trapped between the Cat and the brush cutter, so that when the equipment was raised, the bear simply rode up on the yoke of the brush cutter and stepped off onto the engine hood. The first rule when operating a Cat is that *one* is comfortable, while *two* is very much a crowd!

One cold day, Father was working alongside his friend, Eddy Trudel, cutting and piling brush. While he was overturning tree stumps, Eddy accidentally killed a young black bear that had been frightened from its den. These two mischievous men who were always looking for fun, decided to hide this bear in someone's bed back at camp. The poor unsuspecting fellow that *won* the bear prize was their friend, Gerry Barry. Now, it was Gerry's habit to stay out late, so when he came home singing late in the night, the lights were all out, but the mischief makers were still awake and watching. Gerry happily stripped down and slipped under the covers, but his sweet rest was only momentary. The men who were watching will testify that with a scream of horror, their victim virtually flew from the bed and out of the bunkhouse, reportedly in a single bound! I'm sure that the perpetrators spent the next several hours snickering over their dastardly prank. This became the joke of the winter for the Lassiter boys that year.

When it came to practical jokers, it seemed that no one in the free world was safe, and the next unsuspecting victim would be big Cliff Osterman. Cliff was Cat-skinning west along the Fox Creek, a long way from home. On this dark and overcast night, he became disoriented and missed his shift change back at camp. Now, if his luck wasn't already bad enough, guess who they sent to find him? You've got it, the pranksters, Frank Greenfield and Eddy Trudel. Cliff had stopped along the banks of Fox Creek and had built a fire in front of his dozer blade in order to keep warm.

Alone in the quiet of the wilderness, he relaxed and waited for daylight to arrive, unaware of the approaching danger. When his rescuers spotted the campfire in the distance, they were barely able to

33

believe their good fortune. Covering their flashlights with a cloth, the two men sneaked quietly up on the unsuspecting camper as he snoozed by the fire. What an opportunity! Out of the inky darkness, Dad and Eddy rushed the campfire, growling fiercely, which sent Cliff screaming over backwards, down into the ravine behind him. Only a large tree prevented him from descending the full three hundred feet down the bank and into the creek! With wide grins and flashlights uncovered, the two *jokers* now had a real rescue on their hands, as they clambered downhill after their frightened friend. The truth, of course, was that if they hadn't jumped Cliff when he least expected it, the two jokers would not likely have succeeded. Cliff was a veritable mountain of a man who was more than capable of defending himself in the face of danger.

Monster machines open the land

The Lassiter crews worked day and night on those noisy, rough contraptions. The D8s were monster machines, virtually devoid of suspension, causing them to pound harshly over every log and frozen stump. The young men were hardy, strong, and of high endurance, who, for only a dollar an hour, endured gruelling 12-hour shifts in the cold of winter and the heat of summer. They dutifully worked to cut down that immense forest and pile the brush to be burned. After the brush was cleared and burned, they employed those same Cats to pull enormous tillers that prepared the land for agriculture. The homesteader could then come in and begin finishing the fields with smaller equipment, some even drawn by horses.

With the bulk of the trees removed and the hardest part of the land broken up, the homesteader needed only to finish removing the tree roots that were still lurking in the soil, and cultivate the land.

Root picking, however, was a job that employed most families for years to come. Tree roots, hidden in the soil, would present any number of problems for the farmer, such as getting caught in harvesting machines or causing their cultivating equipment to leap out of the ground. The tedious removal of this underground menace turned out to be a backbreaking and dirty job. As youngsters, we all became intimately familiar with the skill of root picking, and wealthy was the homesteader who had many children to help with the work.

Although it was hard work, we all knew that it was a necessary step to develop our family farm. Everywhere one travelled in those days, there were farms with rows and rows of these little root piles lining the fields. Once burned, these dirty piles would smoulder away sometimes for days as the farmer attempted to eliminate them. This created a haze of pungent root pile smoke across the land, a smell that I will never forget.

Every half-section homestead was bordered with a 20-rod strip (about 100 meters) of bush down the east side and across the south end. This was an effective method of protecting the land from wind erosion and the spread of blowing weed seeds. Most landowners would eventually remove this bush by hand, but at the time, it served as a good windbreak and a ready supply of firewood, berries and mushrooms. These little strips of bush also lessened the impact that civilization had upon the wildlife in the area, giving them corridors of freedom. In this way, it also helped the early pioneers who depended upon this wild meat for survival.

Enjoying the bounty

Indeed, in this newly claimed land, wildlife was in abundance, providing great hunting for pioneering youngsters whose job it was to keep the larder supplied with fresh partridge or rabbits.

We were all accustomed to seeing coyotes, wolves, porcupine and black bears, as they continually moved through the area. Moose and deer were plentiful as well, and co-existed with our domestic animals, sometimes on the same pastureland. There were even a few elk in our area, which were a preferred game because of their deliciously mild, lean meat.

During the very early days, some hungry families even ate greasy bear meat. Black bear meat is similar to that of pork, and bear grease is much like lard.

Orange capped mushrooms were also an abundant treat. As a family, we would often go tramping through the wet bush after a warm, summer rain in search of these little gems, hurriedly trying to beat the worms to the feast. In summer, tasty white mushrooms would often emerge from under the hard packed surface of the road. These, too, made a delightful dish.

Each year, we could depend on a bountiful supply of berries, which ripened under the hot Alberta sun. Sweet saskatoons, strawberries, blueberries, gooseberries and chokecherries would preserve nicely for winter food supplies. Mother made a selection of jams and jellies as well as sweet wine out of this annual treat. She also used dandelions and beets to extend her wine selection. Every summer, she would mix great crocks full of the most repulsive, fermenting slop you could ever imagine, but in a few weeks the bubbling swill became a sweet tasting wine, ready to be siphoned off into glass one-gallon jugs.

I have often wished that Mom's dandelion wine, in the first stage of extraction, could be marketed as a refreshing pop. If only the alcohol was removed, it was such an extraordinary drink that it could have put Coca-Cola right out of business! Alas, it was reserved for the connoisseur of fine wines to sip in the evening light after a hard day in the field.

These were a few of the treats the land had to offer the hard working farmer, pleasures that helped to break the monotony of the hardships of early life on the Project.

Mr. Lassiter continued to open up this vast bush land well into the early fifties, and by then the Peace Country was teeming with expectant families, eager to carve a future out of the rich land. Most of them began on that scanty half-section, and amazingly, survived and even prospered. In contrast now, over fifty years later, it's not uncommon to find a family struggling to make a living on several *full* sections of land.

This time of hardship and scanty beginnings was the soil in which our parents sowed their dreams, watered them with hope and built their business. Emerging from such rustic surroundings, progress was readily evident after every hard day of work and each month of concentrated labour. Slowly, the dreams took shape, and hope became reality as the bush came under cultivation and farmsteads were established. Thus, this era of *great anticipation* had begun to pay dividends of tangible reality.

Frank Greenfield

Heated with a wood stove, this was winter travelling comfort in Saskatchewan during the 1930's

Chapter
Two

A cool beginning

Crossing the great rivers

Although Canada was finally at peace, unrest and the threat of war was looming in Korea, and the United Nations was preparing a military operation to meet this new threat. Thus, the tragic Korean conflict would soon begin, and many of our Canadian soldiers would again taste the horrors of war.

Meanwhile, Canada was a flurry of activity as the World War Two veterans and many immigrants were scrambling to get established. In northern Alberta, inadequate roads and the absence of bridges across the great rivers made travel difficult for the increased flow of settlers coming into the area. Men and women would have to meet these challenges with great determination in order to overcome and continue.

When farmers wanted to move cattle or horses across one of these rivers, they attempted to cross when the river was at its lowest and quietest time. To relocate a herd from one side to the other, a person would row a small boat across, leading one animal by rope and halter. The rest, when driven into the water, would usually follow without too much difficulty. It was a long swim, but cattle and horses alike would cross this way and eventually climb out on the opposite riverbank some distance down stream from where they entered the water.

Resourceful people had constructed cable ferries at strategic river crossings over which a car could travel. However, these crossings were unreliable and inadequate for the transportation of large equipment.

The ferries, of course, could not operate in winter, forcing travellers to cross these wide rivers on the ice, which was at best, risky. The flowing river water created weak spots in the ice and this, in turn, created some tense moments as people attempted to bring in supplies. Even the army had difficulty, and unfortunately, more than one vehicle fell through. Seasonal changes also restricted river crossings for a few months each year because of floodwater or dangerous ice floes.

People needing to move vehicles and equipment across the Smoky River, near Eaglesham, often sneaked over on the railway bridge when they were certain that the train was not going to catch them in transit. Crossing over a high railway trestle with no side railings and with the wind whistling through the timbers took nerves of steel, but many did and survived. At one point, the Northern Alberta Railway, or the NAR as it was called, placed sharp spikes on the bridge ties to deter this action. Ingenuity prevailed, however, and men simply laid large planks over the spikes and continued on.

Years later, before the highway bridge was completed at the town of Peace River, people would drive their vehicles across the town railway bridge. The structure was very narrow and long with no side rails. Fearfully, one could see a long way down to the river through the spaces in the ties.

The ferry over the Peace River at Dunvegan was also an adventurous crossing, and was notorious for slipping its cables and going on safari for miles down stream! On occasion when this happened, someone had to rescue it with a powerful boat and bring everyone back. Telephones did not exist that far north in those days, so it often took a while before anyone noticed that the ferry was missing!

Father continued to work each day with the Lassiter crew clearing land on the Project. Eddy Trudel, who was a surveyor and a good friend, had suggested to him that he seriously consider a particularly rich area of land northwest of town along the Fox Creek. So it was, that while clearing that land by Cat and preparing this homestead for agriculture, Dad found that the soil was indeed a rich, black loam and excellent for growing crops.

An atmosphere of optimism

This was an exciting time in the lives of my folks! Life was beginning to take shape and dreams were materializing. It was 1947, and in the news this year, Canada had reached a population of fourteen million people, and was growing by over one hundred thousand a year through immigration. Newfoundland was being considered as the tenth Canadian province under the Liberal leadership of Prime Minister Louis St. Laurent.

This was also an exciting time in Canada's history and I was born in February 1950, in just such an atmosphere of optimism. Like most northern winters, it was a bitter cold day when it came time for Mother to rush to the hospital. The old Dodge needed to have warm oil poured into the engine and the radiator filled with water. A charged, warm battery was carried from the house and soon they were able to start the old car and head out on snowy roads for the town of Grande

Prairie. That was, no doubt, a harsh three-hour trip on narrow roads through the swirling snow, but it seemed warm enough to me! The thermometer dove to minus forty-five degrees that night when Mom brought me into the world, *but we all have to start somewhere.* Dad spent a restless night in a three-dollar motel and left the car in a local garage all night so that it wouldn't freeze up. The next day, with Mom and me comfortable in the hospital, Father dashed for home again in a swirling blizzard to get back to work. Mom and I came home after a warm stay in the hospital and spent a quiet winter in our little cabin in Eaglesham.

Carving out the farmstead

Spring eventually came to the Peace Country much the way it does every year, in a swirl of melting snow and delicate spring colours. It was 1950, and Billie Holiday was singing "My Foolish Heart" while Bing Crosby had just aired "Dear Hearts and Gentle People" on the radio. For my folks that year, every available day off during the summer and fall was spent preparing the fields and the farmyard site out on the homestead.

In the Peace Country, streets and roadways were constructed of wonderful, hard packed clay, which made superb building material *when it was dry.* When rained upon, it became a very sticky mud that we called "gumbo." This extremely adhesive mud seemed to stay with you like an old friend; it stuck to your boots, rolled up on your vehicle tires and found its way inside your clothing. Many a time, I have taken a great step over a puddle, to discover in horror that the gumbo had extracted my rubber boot! At this point, you find yourself knee deep in the cold muck in your sock feet. Only losing one's boot in the same gooey mixture in the middle of the smelly barnyard could top that thrill!

There were few developed roads in the area, so an access to each farmyard site had to be carved out of the dense boreal forest by the farmer himself. The few roads that did exist were relatively new and not well developed. There was little or no gravel over the clay grade, so it was a common occurrence after a rain to find oneself stuck right in the *middle* of the road.

Our little community was, however, becoming more established each year with roads, stores, a new hotel and this year, the construction of a new school.

Meanwhile, our little farm was also developing. The access to that homestead was simply a trail that had been bulldozed by Cat through the bush to where our little house would eventually rest. Before the snow melted in the spring of '51, plans were made to move our house from town, out to the farm.

To do this, Dad procured a D8 Cat from Mr. Lassiter to plough the snow off the roadway, and to haul our little shack those five frosty miles out to the farmstead. He chose this particular time to move, because those early shacks were built upon log skids that would drag easily along on the frozen ground. This was a move that would be impossible during spring break-up because of the muddy roads.

Once Dad had the little house chained up to the Cat and was preparing to leave, a neighbour came to say, "Hey Frank, would you be able to tow mine along behind yours?" "Well, Bruce" he said, "I have the power, so sure, why not?" No sooner had he chained that little house on, when two more Eaglesham neighbours discovered the opportunity and also asked to be added to the train!

Just like my parents, these neighbours had all been preparing their farms while working elsewhere, so it was, that many of them were ready for a spring move. Each homesteader, however, lacked the means to make that essential move. So, by the time Dad had gone from one end of town to the other, he had no less than four little shacks chained onto his D8 Cat, one behind the other. Now, this isn't a huge job for a Cat that size, but keeping them all in a straight line between the high snow banks would prove to be a challenge!

Reportedly, some of the homeowners rode along in their homes on that Cat train, keeping the wood stove stoked and the house warm. That would have been a rare site; a big old Caterpillar tractor clattering down the frozen road, sending a plume of white exhaust into the cold northern air. And, following close behind were four little cabins, some with smoke trailing from their chimneys. Upon closer scrutiny, one might even have noticed excited faces peering out the windows!

Soon after they had turned north from the correction line road, someone came running from behind, frantically waving their arms and screaming, "Stop, stop!" Dad throttled back and hauled the big Cat out of gear. The skid logs had pulled out from under Peggy Gartly's house. after it caught the snow bank, damaging the building and leaving furniture and affects spread all over the road. Considering all the things that could have gone wrong that day, they were fortunate that only this one mishap occurred.

Dad unhooked the houses one by one as they came to their respective farmsteads, then continued on to travel the final three miles to our own little clearing in the bush by the creek. That was truly an historic and demanding day in the life of my parents.

Mrs. Gartly's home had to be repaired while most of her belongings were piled safely on the snow banks. Sometime later, while unpacking, she found that the towels and bedding had been exposed just long enough for the roadside mice to enter and leave their little calling cards.

Eventually, everyone's little cabin arrived on a pre-planned spot, ready to establish their home, their family and their dreams. That must have been a lonely start, as families would have been isolated from town and neighbours for a full month during spring break up. The Alberta government had yet to build side roads, so only the main highways and survey roads existed. This meant that reliable travel depended upon dry, good weather or upon frozen ground.

The Department of Veterans Affairs offered a meagre $2,300 to initiate the homestead. For most people, that is all the working capital they would have, and frugally purchased their first necessities with that grant.

Government of the Province of Alberta

Announcements of Plans for Establishment of Veterans on Provincial Lands

LANDS available for disposition to veterans by the Department of Lands and Mines, are divided into four classes. However, no disposition of land will be made till there has been a soil investigation to determine that the land is suitable for the growing of crops. Application for land should be made at the Provincial Land Office. Provincial Land Offices are located at Edmonton, Calgary, Peace River and Sub-Agency Offices at Grande Prairie, Bonnyville, Hines Creek, Lac La Biche and Rocky Mountain House.

Provincial Lands Other Than School Lands

A veteran can obtain 320 acres of land under the Agricultural Lease regulations, irrespective of his other holdings. Application should be made at the Provincial Lands Agency for the district in which the land desired is situated. When application is made the land is immediately placed under reservation for the veteran until the soil investigation is made and when the report is received immediate consideration is given to the application and the veteran advised of the decision.

Under the Agricultural Lease the veteran pays no crop share during the three years following the granting of the lease, unless there has been an area previously cultivated; thereafter he pays to the province a one-eighth share of all crops grown on the land as rent and taxes. (He has no other charges to pay.) In any year when the average yield of crops harvested is less than 5 bushels per acre, no crop share is payable.

When a veteran has completed the requirements of the lease in each of 10 years, he may receive, upon making application, title to the land or he may carry on under the terms of the lease.

Lands Cleared and Broken

The Government has entered into a contract for clearing and breaking of lands covered by brush and timber. These lands will be made available to veterans under regulations similar to the Agricultural Lease regulations with the exception that the veteran will have to deliver to the province in each year for 7 years, subsequent to the issue of the lease, a one-third share of all crops grown on the land as rent and taxes. (He has no other charges to pay.) Arrangements will be made whereby the veteran will receive title at the end of 10 years, providing he has complied with the terms of the lease.

Lands Requiring Irrigation

At the present time certain proposed irrigation projects are being investigated and if found feasible and work is undertaken for the development of the project the Provincial lands within the irrigation project will be made available by sale at the nominal price of $10.00 to veterans on the basis of a maximum of 160 acres to an applicant. Under this arrangement the veteran will be required to pay all taxes, water rates and other charges assessed against the land. (There are no lands at present available.)

School Lands

Veterans who were residents of Alberta at the time of enlistment can obtain under the Agricultural Lease regulations a maximum of 320 acres. (Lands already held under lease are not available for disposition.) As many of these lands are situated in settled areas the acreage obtainable will depend upon the location and shall be in the discretion of the Minister.

No lease shall be issued for these lands until after the 15th of April, 1946, and in the meantime applications will be accepted from eligible veterans. When making disposition of the land preference will be given to veterans residing within the district in which the land is situated and when there is more than one application for the same parcel of land disposition will be made at a drawing to take place after the aforesaid date. Where no preference is granted and more than one application is received for the same parcel of land disposition will be made at a drawing to take place after the aforesaid date. No application will be accepted for school land from a veteran who is already the owner of a farm in fee simple or holds farm lands under an Agreement of Sale. The Minister shall settle as he deems best all disputes which may arise between persons claiming the right to lease the same land.

All types of Agricultural Leases will require that the veteran reside upon the land or in the immediate vicinity, as provided in the regulations. When making application the veteran must deliver to the Agent of Provincial Lands a certificate from one of the Regional Offices, Soldier Settlement and Veterans' Land Act, certifying that he is a veteran within the meaning of The Veterans' Land Act, 1942 (Canada).

A person wishing financial assistance under The Veterans' Land Act will have to be qualified by the Regional Committee pursuant to The Veterans' Land Act.

Application for financial assistance or for a certificate certifying that he is a veteran, should be directed to the Regional Office in the district in which the land is situated. Offices of the Soldier Settlement and Veterans' Land Act have been set up at: Lethbridge, Calgary, Red Deer, Edmonton, St. Paul, Grande Prairie and Peace River.

EDMONTON, ALBERTA.
September 17th, 1945.

HON. N. E. TANNER,
Minister of Lands and Mines.

Veteran Land Agreement 1945

My parents spent their grant money wisely, and purchased a two cylinder A.R. John Deere tractor, a six ft. seeder and disk, as well as a tiller and harrows to work the land with. The construction of a *dugout* pond, which would provide them a plentiful, renewable water supply, was also squeezed out of that initial allowance. They used their 1928 Dodge car for transportation and hauling until enough money could be made to purchase their first truck the following year. Father would inform friends that he owned, not a Dodge, but a *Rolls*. "Yes," he would say, "it is a 'Rolls Canardly.' It rolls down the hills but can 'ardly make it up the other side."

From hope to prosperity

You might wonder by now, *just what was the point* of expending all that energy, moving into the wilderness and often risking life and limb to do it? *What on this green earth was the attraction?* What in the world would make people leave civilization and move to the bush?

Clearly, to an adventurous heart, it was the chance to claim free or at least relatively free land, in the form of a homestead. Back on the prairies, one had to work for many a hard year to save up enough money to buy a 320-acre farm. But here, little cash was required; only an extra large measure of guts and tenacity was needed to establish a viable farming business. So, with a strong back and a strong community spirit, this land was whipped and tamed for human use.

I cannot imagine how hard my parents had to work to cultivate enough land, pull the stubborn stumps, then

48

pick and burn the roots to be able to plant that first 100 acres of oats. But, the work paid off, and they were rewarded that fall with a bumper crop of Victory Oats at 100 bushels to the acre! This was a very prosperous increase even by today's standards, and started us out in grand style. The yield was so high that Dad had to hire neighbours and friends to come and help with the harvest. Not having enough grain storage, he deposited a huge pile of oats on the ground, surrounded by a chicken wire fence, backed with tarpaper. By the time it was all shipped out, Father had sold a whole railway grain car full of oats from that one field alone, which is amazing when one considers that the largest farm implement we had was only six feet wide!

With this financial boost, Mom and Dad were able to purchase a Chevy half-ton pickup truck and a badly needed Humming Bird brand threshing machine for processing the next year's harvest. The threshing machine, a forerunner to the modern combine, would be used to separate the grain from the straw as the crops were harvested.

Wildlife opposition

Even as an infant, I had a chance to help out. Yes, still in my daybed, I acted as a decoy for the hungry mosquitoes while my parents laboured in the garden. The job paid only room and board, but kept me quite busy during the long summer days.

As a little tot, I have only shadow-like memories of being carried along from the barn to the chicken pen, to the garden. Mom carried me everywhere, talking with me as she went. Our conversations were decidedly one-sided at first, as I just watched and listened, but she spoke to me not as a child, but as she would to an adult. I see now, that because my folks spoke to me in adult talk, my vocabulary matured more quickly than that of some other children at the time.

My parents had chosen a wonderful, scenic point of land as a building site for our home, looking north over the Fox Creek. It was a picturesque yard site indeed, but if it had a drawback, it was the fact that its location was along a major game corridor. My first real clear memories are of being roughly scooped up by my mother as she dashed into our little house. "Frankie!" she called, "it's another bear!" *Frankie* really had nothing but a small .22 calibre rifle in those days, which would hardly fend off a menacing bear, but he was formidable with a shovel!

Indeed, we didn't have to travel far to experience observable wildlife, needing only to peer quietly through the windows of our little house. There were countless black bear following the creek side, hungry moose and deer to nibble on the garden, and a myriad of furry rodents to make life interesting. Possibly, they had heard that "possession is 9/10ths of the law" and were asserting their claim as native creatures in the land.

At any rate, my parents, being ambitious human entrepreneurs, were not to be dissuaded. Little by little, the farm took shape and developed into a viable agricultural enterprise. Side by side, they shared the rigorous physical challenges that accompany such a grass roots venture, and daily they were rewarded by the beauty and the richness of the land.

Much to my mother's horror, I had discovered the joy of exploration by the time I was two years old. She caught me one day in the spring of '52 trying to negotiate the log bridge that Dad had built across the swirling creek. "Where do you think you're going!" she hollered over the roar of the creek. "Goin' to help Daddy!" I called back from the middle of the bridge. This resulted in a period where exploration was somewhat restricted. In fact, I felt lucky to be able to peer outside through the crack in the door. Not for long, though, because life on the farm was an outdoor life. If we weren't working the land or tending the animals, we were picking mushrooms or building something under the warm summer sun.

The farm business steadily grew, and so did I. Our vegetable garden was small at first, and had to be supplemented with wild greens growing on this virgin land. At mealtimes, we often boiled a pot of fresh wild pigweed, which renders a kind of spinach-like vegetable. Dandelions also make a nice wild salad when picked fresh and young. Recognizable common vegetables would replace these as the garden developed, but I shall always remember the unique flavour of some of the nice wild plants. Desserts were easier, with delicious wild strawberries, gooseberries or saskatoons.

Eventually, corrals and pens were built to house our pigs and chickens, and a pole barn was built for the cattle. In the absence of lumber at the time, Father had to cover the pole framework of the barn with straw to shed the water. His barn looked more like a giant straw igloo, but this crude and simple structure served us for a good many years and proved to be a warm and practical shelter for the cattle.

One of Father's first farm inventions was the *portable pigpen*. Most farm pens in the area were permanent, made by fence posts driven into the ground. The hogs, however, would soon excavate this type of pen, leaving absolutely nothing but a mud hole to live in. With a portable pen, however, the pigs always had new grass and clean dirt to dig in. The pen was constructed with a log base around the bottom and the pig house and fence were up on top of the logs. One had only to hook onto it with the tractor once a week and move it a few feet ahead onto new ground. In this way, we always had happy little pigs on fresh green grass. The second advantage was, that wherever the pen had been placed, the pasture grew in fertile abundance. With each invention, addition or hard day's work, our agricultural endeavour grew and prospered.

A move to safety

In addition to living on a game corridor, we discovered yet another disadvantage of having our home so near the creek. In summer, the standing water in the creek became an immense breeding ground for mosquitoes. This, of course, meant constant exercise with no rest until one was safely under the covers at night! Thankfully, a few years later, some clever person invented insect repellent, but at the time, we were left to our homemade remedies and wildly waving arms.

The third and final disappointment of our new home location occurred when spring arrived, and the creek suffered spring break-up. The crashing ice floes and high water produced an uncomfortable situation and constant worry that the yard site could be undermined and slip into the torrent. This last discovery led to the decision to move our little cabin away from the creek and further into the bush.

In the spring of 1954, my parents prepared a new yard site a safe 400 yards from the creek banks, and the move was accomplished with the willing help of our neighbours. On moving day, Dad's John Deere tractor was chained to the log skids that were under our little house, then a couple of neighbours respectively chained their tractors ahead of ours, and the pull began. It was my job to balance the bookcase so it couldn't topple over, and so, got to ride in the moving cabin as it bumped and jerked along the bush trail to its new resting site. This proved to be a good job to keep a four-year-old out of harm's way.

My folks had made a wise decision, as being just that much further from the creek banks relieved some of the rigours of northern life. This new site, though not as scenic as the other, was much more practical and had more room for outbuildings and a larger garden.

Good healthy food

The following spring, Mother lovingly went to work building a vegetable garden that today would be called a *mini farm!* Carved out of the raw bush, this plot would dependably feed our family for the next eighteen years.

Throughout the years, I spent many hot days and mosquito-infested evenings in that garden. Though I hated the work, I loved the produce, and there was always something wonderful and satisfying about gathering the vegetable harvest and storing it for winter. By this, I learned that good things seldom come without hard work. Father Matthew Record once penned, "There aren't any rules for success that will work unless *you* do" and the farm afforded many good examples of this valuable principle. I have never tasted such wonderful vegetables since then, and am forever thankful for the good healthy food I had to grow up on.

Each May, we dutifully planted long rows of peas and carrots, onions, beets, corn and other veggies. Mom loved her cauliflower, parsnip and cabbage, and many hills of potatoes were also planted. By July each year, the garden was high with corn and sunflowers. With a lot of weeding and care, we could look forward to a bountiful harvest that would feed us through the winter.

During the harvest, mother slaved for long hours over the hot wood-fired cook stove to preserve our produce in one-quart sized sealing jars (a bit larger than a litre). Electricity would eventually make this chore a lot easier, but for many years, our only method of preserving food would be in sealed glass jars. Every vegetable was carefully cleaned, diced and boiled in a canner on the stove. When the jars were removed from the hot water, lids were attached with new rubber sealer rings. The cooling of the jars produced a near vacuum inside, protecting the produce from bacteria and decay. Even meat (chicken, beef, pork or moose) was cut in small chunks and canned as preserves. A jar of canned meat was enough to feed the whole family for a meal or two. It was very tender and tasted delicious.

We were also in the process of developing a herd of cattle, so of course one shouldn't *eat the profits*, if possible. Consequently, good healthy meat to feed our family had to come from some other source. This left only the hunting of wild game or fowl. Moose meat and venison was readily available, tasty, lean and healthy and I think most farm kids in those years grew up on heaping platefuls of fresh farm potatoes, garden vegetables and wild meat.

On occasion, Dad would butcher a pig and mix the pork with the moose when it was processed. The dry, lean moose, mixed with the more fatty pork, made a wonderfully flavoured mix that was a real treat (at least at the beginning of the season). The challenge was then Mother's, to invent new and tasty ways of preparing moose burger for endless suppers.

Nurtured by the land

Living on the edge of the bush, far from what seemed like anywhere, was a lonely, remote existence, but I am thankful to have experienced that lifestyle. Had I been raised in some great metropolis of bustling society, there would never have been a chance to experience what only the land can teach you. Patience could never have been learned so well as when we were waiting for spring crops and gardens to grow, or when watching quiet wildlife. Ingenuity can be learned while patiently watching industrious beaver at work building their lodges or dams, or when spying on spring birds engineering their nests (not to mention watching Mom and Dad conquering the many challenges of homestead life).

Certainly, one can never learn to appreciate the value and enjoyment of sheer silence until you sit stock still on a snowy day, observing a peaceful deer feeding in the forest. I don't believe that anyone can hope to appreciate what northern nature really has to offer, until every season is enjoyed in the beauty of the great outdoors.

Chapter
Three

A cabin under the
northern lights

Having travelled half way around the world in my lifetime, I have seen every conceivable type of dwelling, from grass huts on the South Sea Islands, to great mansions on the hills overlooking Hollywood. Experiencing everything from the scorching heat of an Australian desert to the monsoon rains of Polynesia, my heart is still most at home in Canada's north. Possibly, I am a hopeless romantic, but even while sun tanning on the famous Bondi Beach near Sydney, Australia, I would close my eyes and visualize our little home in the north, all banked with powdery snow on a cold winter's night. Overhead, the Northern Lights would sweep in colourful bars of green, yellow and red, as our windows glowed with soft lantern light. Seasonal extremes and the vibrancy of life in the northland will somehow etch its imprint on the human heart for life, as it surely did on mine.

The first northern homes were only cabins or shacks, but were movable, practical and affordable. The skid logs under the shack kept the home up out of the dirt and water, and left a necessary air space under the floor to prevent the building from rotting. In winter, the home had to be banked with snow all the way around to prevent the frigid northern air from blowing under the floor. While not as efficient as a modern insulation, this method was still quite effective. There was something wonderfully romantic about cabin living. The creature comforts were not always present, but it was affordable shelter and fit the need of the day.

Our cabin under the Northern Lights

Our first buildings on the farm were constructed of shiplap lumber. To keep out the wind and rain, each board was cleverly overlapped by the one above. Then, to further deter the elements, the outside walls of our home were covered by a practical material much like rolled roofing. This covering on our little shack gave it the appearance of grey brick construction, and was a modern exterior cladding at the time.

Board floors were common in every cabin and proved very practical. Living out on the land meant that your boots were always loaded with samples of the last place you walked, and upon entering the house, some of these particles got left behind on the kitchen floor. Barn boots were the exception, having been carefully scraped off or left outside. With this early type of flooring, a simple broom was all that was needed to remove the dirt and other nefarious particles back out the door again.

If the lumber hadn't been adequately dried before the building was constructed, it would usually shrink and leave handy spaces in the floor through which the dirt could be easily expelled. Because of these natural openings, we almost always had a mousetrap set to catch little fuzzy rodents before they found their way to the oatmeal. When they did persist in attempting to join our household, they were bound to meet my mother, the pest exterminator! It was indeed pure entertainment, watching Mom with broom in hand and an unswayable determination, trying to catch one of these panic-stricken creatures.

Another useful and simple feature of our home was the inside walls that were also constructed out of lumber. These could suffer intense abuse without much apparent damage. This, I recall, was a definite advantage in the heat of wooden sword fights or wrestling matches. One could also drive a common nail absolutely anywhere without having to find a hidden stud. Hence, there were nails for coat hangers, nails for calendars, nails for pictures, and spikes to hang larger items such as the rifle or tools.

Over the oil or wood stove, there would always be some type of drying rack suspended from the ceiling, a simple device that proved to be a very useful and economical dryer for wet clothing.

Illumination by lantern

Inevitably, there was also a steel hook, usually screwed through the middle of a large automobile hubcap in the ceiling above the kitchen table. This was where the gas lantern hung that provided light and even some heat for the entire house. The hubcap served as an inexpensive safety shield to keep the ceiling from catching fire from the heat of the lantern.

These lanterns were fuelled with high-test gasoline, which was pressurized with a little hand pump on the lamp. They provided a bright, white light, as the fuel burned inside of silk mantles. Like the ticking of an old clock, the calm hiss of the gas lantern late in the evening was a soothing sound for tired little ears. These lanterns had the added versatility of being portable, so if you required a light somewhere else on the farm, you could quickly lift it down from the kitchen ceiling and carry it away.

A portable light more commonly used in those days was a coal oil lamp. They were smaller and could be carried easily from room to room. Coal oil lamps offered quite enough light to read by, and were simple and practical. Coal oil, which is like kerosene, did not burn as clean as a gas lantern and emitted an oily residue, which eventually appeared as a sooty film on windows and ceilings.

On dark winter nights, we even lit the barn with one of these simple oil lamps. It hung on a wall mount and

61

had a metal reflector behind the chimney to deflect the light, giving just enough light to milk the cows by. One had to be careful with any of these lamps, as the glass globes (or chimneys) were hot to the touch and very breakable. Many a pioneer home was burned to the ground because of a lantern accident.

Cabin practicality

Our little cabin was the most simple and practical dwelling I've ever had the pleasure to live in. I always liked the soothing sound of a warm summer rain on the roof, and our little home seemed to be constantly filled with the friendly aromas from the wood cook stove. Delightful smells, such as freshly baked bread or hot saskatoon pie tease my memory to this day. Despite its hominess, however, I recall that my parents could barely wait to replace this rustic little cabin with a more modern home, but we would have to wait another ten years for that.

The old house held other dear memories, like those cold winter nights when the mercury plummeted out of sight in the thermometer! Since the walls were insulated only with wood shavings, the "R" value insulating factor diminished with the age of the structure. This happens as a result of moisture collecting in the shavings, causing them to settle over time. So it was, that on a cold morning, one could readily detect where the level of insulation was in any given wall by the frost line on the *inside* of the wall!

When the outside temperature dropped suddenly, as it often does in the North Country, the nails in the walls would jump out a little. This made a popping sound that would add to the symphony of creaking and groaning sounds also caused by the cold. Consequently, this became our weather barometer, in that, while sitting in the comfort of the oil or wood stove, one could fairly accurately interpret changes in the weather by the sounds the old house made.

On days when we were pinned down by the cold weather for a period of time and the door was kept closed to keep out the storm, moisture would build up on the windows so thick that it was futile to attempt its removal. The cold crept through the walls anywhere it could, and from each nail head on the walls furthest from the stove, clung a little ball of frost. These little white studs decorated the house in a most unusual manner and added to our unique northern décor.

My little bedroom was at the opposite end of the house from my parents' bedroom, separated only by the kitchen. It was the furthest room from the stove, and for at least one month each winter, my blankets were permanently frozen to the outside wall. When I could not sleep, I would lie in bed and draw patterns in the frost on the wall by my feather pillow.

Of course, the cold temperature was never as serious for the *little pioneers*, as we were not responsible for outside chores. We were never required to tumble out of bed onto frozen floors at 6:00 A.M. to do farm chores like our parents had to, at least not for the first few blissful years of our lives.

A rough experience

The greatest advantage of being a child was in not being required, during cold or wet weather, to make the trek out to the outhouse on the other side of the yard. We had our own little handy potty that was kept warm in the bedroom. Adults, on the other hand, often waited until they could stand the strain no longer before dashing madly through the swirling snow to the *biffy*. The point at which this custom is transformed from routine into an adventure, is when one has consumed too much coffee the night before, and the outhouse call comes at 4:00 A.M! (I believe the chamber pot was invented for such emergencies.)

The pages of the Eaton's catalogue, which faithfully served as toilet paper, did not get any softer as the temperature dropped, resulting in a *rough* experience! Visitors from the city with soft bums often took exception to our recycling the catalogue in this way. But think about it for a moment. Where else could one pause and think, read a little, place an order for new blue jeans and then use the pages for cleanup? It was obviously the initiative of deeply profound and insightful minds, wouldn't you agree?

Some may think it a great hardship not having indoor plumbing, but there is an advantage. This was realized on those particularly crisp mornings when you arose to find that the oil stove had gone out, last night's dishwater was frozen in the pan, your long-johns were frozen on the rack and your boots were too stiff to get into. This was the time to be thankful that the water pipes were not frozen, only because *there were no pipes!*

Daily, water for various uses was carried in by hand. When the water became dirty and required draining out, one merely flung the contents of the basin or bucket out the door. Of course, it was always prudent to first check to see if the walkway was clear!

Wrigglers for lunch

Our water supply in the dugout became increasingly smellier as the winter went on. With two or three feet of ice covering the pond, natural aeration was diminished, causing the water to become dark and stagnant. There was also a growth of naturally occurring fauna in the water in the form of little wrigglers. Visitors from the city would often refuse a cup of *dugout* coffee simply because of the little cooked wrigglers floating on top. My dad would calmly announce that this was our most consistent supply of protein, and he would continue to sip away, but the general routine was to remove the scum from the water before proceeding.

During the summer, farm days consisted of long hours, often from six in the morning until sunset. For northerners, this meant sixteen or eighteen hours of labour, for by mid-June the sun was still in the sky at 11:30 pm! The late sunset allowed for a great amount of business to be accomplished during those crucial growing months.

Bright crisp winters

By the winter solstice in mid-December, however, the reverse was true, and we experienced very short days and long, long nights. This allowed hard working homesteaders a chance to recover from a summer of physical exhaustion and sleep depravity. One still had to rise early to feed milk-cows and other stock, but after the barnyard chores were completed, there was more time to relax and enjoy family life.

Farm chores did, however, get one outside in a veritable winter wonderland, but there was always the warmth of the house to escape to when you could no longer feel your toes! Alberta is famous for its clear blue winter skies and sun so bright that you can barely open your eyes. After a fresh snowfall, the whole land was covered with a brilliant, white sparkling powder, and the natural beauty of the scene helped you forget the hardship of the cold.

Northern air is often so still when it is very cold, that sound carries a remarkably long distance. Morris and Edie Burroughs lived with their family a mile and a half west of our farm. From our house, on a crisp winter morning, I could clearly hear Morris walk out on his front step and set the milk pails down in the snow. I could hear him speak to his farm dog and hear the crunch of his feet on the frozen path as he made his way to the barn for morning chores.

We could plainly hear the train coming into the Eaglesham station five miles away, and the sound of the cars closing up as the engineer applied the brakes. The sounds of a tractor working or a truck travelling two or more miles away was as clear on a cold winter day as if it were only across the yard.

I can recall my Uncle Bob recounting a story about having shot at a moose one winter, that was not far off the road allowance. The moose went down like he was on an elevator and Bob smiled with pride, slung his rifle over his shoulder and headed for his catch. A moment later, to his surprise, the moose leaped to his feet and crashed off into the bush on the dead run without looking back. Uncle Bob stood there, dumbfounded and disappointed, but soon found what had happened. His careful aim, to diminish the chance of spoiling any meat, was just an inch too high. The all too careful shot had blown an antler right off, which caused the animal's temporary unconsciousness and the reason for its sudden escape.

Bob rested under a great spruce tree and listened as the startled animal crashed blindly through the forest on that cold morning. He recalls hearing the moose break out of the bush a full two miles away, and there was a quiet moment while it crossed the road before more crashing could be heard again in the bush. In the thick air of summer, of course, one would never be able to hear much beyond a couple of hundred yards.

The clear, cold air was only one of many unique characteristics of the northern winter. The pleasant crunch of the snow under my boots was also an enjoyable sound, and is something that I still enjoy today. That sound and the feel of the snow would often change as the day progressed from a crisp, dry morning to a sunny afternoon.

Little fellows love to follow along in the bright snow, trying desperately to jump from one of their father's footprints to another. Once one is exhausted from jumping footprints, you simply fall backward and make snow angels or enjoy the sunlight sparkling in the frosty tree branches.

Living far from a city does grant a quieter lifestyle, so that the natural sounds of the world become much more intimate in one's daily life. The sweet song of a Chickadee bouncing along a snow covered branch, or the welcoming call of the migrating geese in the spring and fall were such delights. These were daily pleasures that gave cheer to the hardworking pioneer, and indelibly imprinted the music of the northland upon our memories.

One cold afternoon, I went on a trip to our neighbours, the Elmquists. I was five years old, and I guess my mother needed a break, so on this sparkling winter day, Dad and I went out to purchase a wagonload of feed wheat. We had a grand visit with Hilding and Frances in their little warm European-style home and enjoyed supper with them before heading home in the dark. The moving tractor created a wind chill of nearly minus 60 degrees that night, so Father had to bury me in the load of grain to keep me from freezing to death on the way. The clear night sky was studded with the most brilliant stars imaginable. Dad drove the John Deere through the snow while I rode in the relative comfort of that wagonload of grain. A scarf covered my face and nose, so only my eyes were left uncovered, with the rest of my snowsuit being covered by the wheat. Part way home, a most delightful light show began, such as I had never seen. The whole sky became alive with brilliant streams of colour that swept across my view. I forgot about the cold. The noisy throb of the tractor faded away and I was somehow immersed in these rivers of spectacular light before me. Since then, I have witnessed the Aurora Borealis many times and have seen extraordinary man-made fireworks and laser light shows, but absolutely none compare to the celestial show I remember that night when I was just a child.

The old copper washtub

Growing up without central heating or indoor plumbing meant that once a week on bath day, everybody shared the same bath water. The big copper tub, hung on a nail on the outside wall, was hauled in and placed in the middle of the kitchen floor. It was then filled with melted snow or dugout water that had been warmed up on the cook stove. Children always got to bath first, then Mother, and last of all, poor old Dad, who doubtless had the most to scrub off. The dirty water was then bucketed back out the door and the tub returned to the spike on the wall. Between weekly baths, we needed to be content with a daily *birdbath* or sponge bath from the enamel basin.

As the farm grew, we eventually graduated to a larger, round galvanized tub, which allowed us greater freedom of movement in the bath. The flat bottom copper tub continued as a container to heat water and wash clothes for many years to come.

The Enterprise cook stove

Our kitchen was graced with an "Enterprise" wood-burning cook stove. This great wood stove had a water container, or reservoir at one end, which provided us with a ready supply of warm water for cleaning or cooking purposes. Each morning, it was filled by bucket either from the dugout during summer, or with fresh snow in winter.

A handy copper dipper hung at the side of the stove and was used to bail the water from the reservoir when needed. These wood or coal burning cook stoves proved to be a very versatile appliance, with a warming oven above the stove and a large baking oven below. There was twice the usable room on that stovetop than on today's electric versions, leaving room for an extra pail of melting snow or several pair of wet mittens to dry. When the stove was used for cooking, the whole house was toasty warm, again a far more economical process than we have today. The Enterprise stove was not always appreciated, however, because when a large meal had to be cooked indoors on a hot summer day, the heat in the house would become almost unbearable.

Every day during winter, fresh firewood had to have the snow knocked off and be carried in and placed in the wood box to warm up. As I grew, splitting and carrying wood became one of my daily chores and helped to build strength and endurance. I recall struggling up the back steps with my arms piled high with snowy firewood, dancing on one foot while kicking my boots off in the porch and then sliding across the kitchen floor on my frozen socks to place the wood near the stove. Mother might turn from her bread dough and holler, "Warren! Next time, sweep the snow off your pants before you come in." I would respond with, "Uhhh, yes Mom...ok, I'll try," thinking to myself, "Oh boy, with an armful of wood, how am I going to do that?"

Washboards to wringer washers

Washday usually filled the house with extra moisture, which the dry wood heat was handy to remove. When I was just a baby, Mom would use a washboard in the copper tub to hand scrub the clothes. These washboards consisted of a wooden frame with a ribbed metal or corrugated glass surface in the middle. The dirty clothing was soaked in the tub full of warm, soapy water, and Mom would vigorously rub the clothes over the washboard until the desired cleanliness was achieved. Extremely greasy coveralls were washed in gasoline first and then washed last in the washtub. Many of the pioneers then boiled the bedding and underwear to ensure that they were free of uninvited crawlies!

Most often, lye soap was used for serious cleaning either on badly soiled coveralls or for washing floors. When used too often, this harsh soap would cause red, raw and cracked hands, so in the early years, goose grease or bear grease was administered as a softening and healing agent. Eventually, the Raleigh dealer, who travelled from farm to farm, provided us with an ointment for this purpose.

As the years progressed and technology evolved, we obtained a Beatty wringer washer for laundry cleaning that Mom would have to wrestle in from the porch on washdays. This new machine would be a great boon to the hardworking farmwoman whose job it was to keep her family clean. A small, Johnston gasoline-engine

71

powered this modern washing machine, with the exhaust pipe vented through a hole in the kitchen wall. Unlike the smooth, electric machines of today, it was a hot, noisy, smelly and sometimes dangerous apparatus to operate. These wringer washers used a powered agitator for washing and rinsing. Then, rather than spinning out the excess water, the clothing was fed carefully between two hard rubber rollers to squeeze the water out. We had to exercise extreme caution when feeding wet clothing into that powerful wringer. It had a nasty way of catching loose clothing, or on painful occasion, one's hand.

These washing machines, brutal as they could be, were a modern marvel compared to the corrugated washboards they replaced. As with the automobile, however, there was often a price to pay for speed and convenience, which sometimes materialized in the form of an accident.

Once, when our family was visiting the Donaldson's home several miles north of us, their neighbour's boy David came screaming into the yard all out of breath. "Mother's hurt, Mother's hurt! She is bleeding!" he cried. Mrs. Donaldson went back with David to the Clemo farm and found that Mrs. Clemo had caught her hand in the wringer washer, which had quickly and painfully extracted her fingernail. My folks stopped in to see Mrs. Clemo on the way home later that day, and while the ladies were visiting, I inspected the evil device and found that it had indeed drawn blood. Life has a way of asserting its more painful lessons even at an early age. An experience like this is enough to make a small boy stuff his hands deep into his pockets and cringe at the thought of parting with a fingernail.

To dry our laundry, we used nature's wind and solar heat to complete the task. Once the washing was wrung out and the laundry stuffed into a basket, it was hauled outside to the clothesline.

We would have all had a good laugh, back then, at the thought of someone actually paying money to dry clothes the way we do today, because nature had provided such an excellent method for free! Kids did not get to hang out clothes until they were tall enough to reach the line and keep the clothing from dragging in the dirt. I fondly remember Mother in her gum rubber boots and skirt out under the clothesline in the mud, trying not to drop the whites. A stream of descriptive words often accompanied the task as mother swatted mosquitoes with one hand and pinned clothes with the other. If the sun was out, the clothes dried quickly; if it rained you sometimes had to leave them out for a day so they could re-dry. In the winter, the clothing froze solid for the first few hours of being outside until the moisture evaporated. Frozen clothes always smelled so wonderfully fresh, that no laundry freshener was ever required.

By nightfall, if the clothes were not completely dry, the frozen garments were pried from the line and brought in to hang near the stove to complete the process. The cabin was often decorated with an array of *undies*, long johns, socks and pants hanging from an indoor clothesline, or draped over chairs. Here again, the dry heat of the wood stove was helpful to remove the extra dampness from the air.

As a little tyke, I remember traipsing out into the kitchen at night and being frightened by all the strange people *hanging around*. Surprisingly, these bizarre people were still around in the morning and I was embarrassed to find that they were just the long johns hung to dry. Occasionally, when a mid-winter storm would last for a couple of weeks or more, our cabin would eventually look like a department store with drying clothing hung up everywhere.

Isolated

The disadvantage in being a kid from the bush is that isolation can leave you lacking in the practical knowledge of the outside world. One day, my uncle Owen arrived for a visit from Edmonton. As I helped him unpack his car, he handed me a banana, which I took straight to my mother and asked, "Mom, can you cook this for me?" Mother broke into a grin, kneeled down and began peeling the strange thing, all the while muttering something about *living in the bush.*

In later years, my cousins and good friends, the Camerons, would visit each May long weekend with my Aunt Dorothy and Uncle Doug. The boys would arrive full of new and strange *city* words and ideas that helped round out my education of the world. After hearing them relate their experiences from the city, however, I believe it made me even more thankful for my remote farm life. My cousins and I were full of fun and energy, bent on exploring the world around us. We exhausted countless hours out along the creek banks or hiding in the haystack. Playing and hunting with our pellet guns, we generally tried to avoid at any cost, being put to work by our mothers.

Farming is a business venture

Being engaged daily with our agricultural venture was an advantage, in that life was very consistent and predictable. Mornings were routinely busy with milking cows, processing the milk, feeding the animals and poultry. Afternoons were filled with other farm work and building projects, then evenings found us again back at the barn with the animals.

Developing a mixed farming operation was an economically wise venture. Specialized farming, on the other hand, was far more prone to failure, simply because there was no other source of backup income. On our mixed farm, we were building a small dairy operation from which we sold milk and cream. We also raised poultry to provide meat and eggs, hogs for meat and sale, and, as well, our grain growing operation. We also grew all of our own feed for the animals, which decreased our overhead costs. This diverse business kept us very busy at home with little time to spend elsewhere.

One of the challenges we faced was in the area of equipment, because such a diverse operation requires a great assortment of machines to complete all the various tasks. This adds to the expense, and also requires the farmer to be well versed in the repair and maintenance of each complex apparatus involved. This fact alone contributed largely to my development in mechanical and electrical understanding, which proved valuable in virtually every career and business of my life.

The administration of such an enterprise was also demanding. Farm animals produce and reproduce as a result of careful feeding and care on the part of the farm manager. This is very critical, especially with a dairy operation that depends upon very specific milking times and practices. For instance, cows will produce the greatest amount and the best quality of milk when milked at exactly the same time every day, without exception. Managing their stress level by keeping them secure and providing a good quality of feed also makes a difference in the quality of their produce. Hence, when *the old man* rouses his son at six in the morning to help milk the cows, there is more to it than the vengeance his son suspects him of.

Grain must be planted, managed and harvested at very specific times to ensure maximum quality, so here again any deviation will cost the farmer precious time and money. Every aspect of farming is similar, in that, strict discipline is required for success. Again, this was a childhood lesson that has aided me all through life because good discipline is vital for success in anything we strive to do.

Our ready cash in those early days came primarily from the sale of cream. Before we could afford a cream separator, the milk had to be left undisturbed in containers for hours until the cream naturally separated and floated to the top. This still seems unscientific to me, simply because cream was thicker and seemed much heavier than milk, so therefore, it should sink instead of floating. Although I excelled in high school science, I never did learn the secret of this anomaly.

As our farm grew more prosperous, Dad finally purchased a hand operated cream separator. This was an economical device that effectively separated the cream from the milk and rendered clean, skimmed milk and rich cream for sale. The Northern Alberta Dairy Pool in Edmonton purchased all the product that our little dairy operation could produce, and paid us in the form of cream cheques issued each month.

My industrious mother soon purchased a one-pound butter press and proceeded to make butter for sale. Without the automated equipment available today, this became a lot of work for the whole family. Working together, we separated the cream, churned the butter, packaged it with N.A.D.P. wrappers and shipped it at precisely the right time so it would not spoil.

Modern coolers would have been a great asset, but of course in those days we had no consistent supply of electricity. Dairy products must naturally be kept from freezing in the winter and from spoiling in the heat of summer. Ingenuity prevailed, and as most early homesteaders did in those days, we used our water well as a cooler. This natural refrigerator kept dairy products fresh and ready for shipping. With a long rope attached to the cream cans, which could be either three or five gallons in size, it took strong arms to lower them in and out of the deep well.

When the train came into the Eaglesham station, the dock was usually cluttered with a long row of cream cans and other packages bound for Edmonton. These would be exchanged with all the empty cans coming back from the creamery, ready to be filled again. After testing the product, the creamery paid on the basis of how clean and fresh each lot was. Number one cream would fetch a handsome $7.00 per five-gallon can as opposed to $2.00 or $3.00 for a lesser quality number two product. Each cream can was required to be sealed with a wire and fitted with a little lead lock through the handle so that the creamery knew which can was fresh. There was always a supply of those little locking devices on the kitchen windowsill that I used to play with as a child.

Each morning and night, Dad and Mom would carry the many large pails of milk back to the house, skim off the bits of straw and other nefarious non-dairy stuff and go through the exercise of separating, churning and preparing the product for sale. It was exercise indeed, as the cream separator itself was enough to play your arms out, not to mention churning butter by hand. Carrying a 16-quart bucket of milk in each hand all the way from the barn to the house also helped to build hard muscles. After the cream was removed, the separator required an extensive cleanup. To do this, we had to disassemble the complicated machine and wash the twenty or so cone shaped disks and apparatus in hot soapy water. You can guess who it was that became very, very adept at that job. On one occasion, I heard, "Warren, get your skinny little butt over here," to which I replied, "I think I'm going to run away!" "Sure you are," Dad announced, "right after you finish the chores!" As I recall, I wasn't the only kid to attempt to negotiate the allotted duties. One day, I overheard my friend Shaun ask his father what he was willing to give him for the chore he was asked to do. Mr. Burroughs, in his infinitely humorous way, retorted, "It isn't what you get when you do the job, Son, it's what you get if you DON'T do it that counts!"

After the cream was separated, the skim milk was used to feed calves and little hungry pigs in the pen. To prepare feed, we used a machine called a chopper that was basically just a grinder, powered by a long belt to the great pulley on the tractor. Dad and I would haul nutritious oats, barley and wheat to mix and grind into a kind of dusty cereal for the animals. This *chop* was then bucketed into wooden troughs for the pigs, and with fresh milk poured over top, it made a kind of porridge that they seemed to really enjoy.

When a good supply of oats was not available, we would mix up a mash of barley and water in a barrel. The water-softened grain became more palatable for the animals and a source of high-energy food. If the barley was left too long in the barrel, however, fermentation would occur and it soon became *pig beer*, which they quite enjoyed, possibly a little too much! I have seen pigs falling all over themselves and acting quite silly after a feed of this potent swill.

To supplement our income, Mother also sold eggs to customers in town, and for years supplied her clients with these farm fresh nuggets. The reason that Mother's eggs were so popular was that they were always squeaky clean, which was rare, as most available farm eggs needed to have the chicken manure washed off before using! Mom also invented a handy egg candler that she had designed to inspect each egg for blood spots or other impurities. This was a wooden box with a small egg shaped hole and a light under it. As the eggs were passed over the light, we could readily see any blemishes and remove those eggs unfit for sale.

Humour in the old corral

When we received a visit from the young United Church student minister visiting in the area, Dad took him on a tour of the farmyard. As we arrived at the pigpen, Dad poured a bucket of leftover food slop and milk into the pig trough. This caused a flurry of snorting, squealing and intense slurping noises as the pigs fought each other for this succulent mix. The poor young man just stood there in absolute unbelief as he surveyed this foul display. My dad peered curiously at him and asked, "Are you alright?" In a few moments, he drew his eyes off of the snorting animals and said to us, "Umm, my father often told me when I was a boy that I ate like a pig. Dear Lord, I didn't know it would be like this!" Dad winked at me and told the young fellow that he would get over it. At any rate, I think this experience contributed to his rather reserved manner at the dinner table that night.

One spring, when I was small, I was standing on the back step of the house with my mother while she was calling the dogs for their supper. My six-foot-two-inch father came striding up from the barn in his usual way with our farm cat on his shoulder and two enormous pails of fresh, foamy milk in his hands. Dad arrived at the gate, and instead of setting the pails down in the mud, he simply stepped over the fence, as he was accustomed to doing when both hands were full. One long leg came gliding over, and in fluid motion, Father turned and lifted the other one to clear the fence. This was a well-practiced routine that would not normally require him to even break stride. That is, until that fateful day when his coveralls got hooked on the top wire of that barbed wire fence. While still in forward motion, but now facing backward with one leg hopelessly caught on the fence, Dad plummeted into the spring muck with both pails of milk held up in the air!

I learned the value of our product that day from Dad, because despite the tumble, he didn't spill much milk. There he lay on his back, in the mud and water, with the two large pails held high off the ground and one leg hung up on the fence! I thought my mother would die of asphyxiation before she was able to stop laughing. She was down on the back step on her hands and knees, snorting and weeping while Dad was cursing a blue streak, trying to get her to come and rescue the milk pails and unhook him from the wire.

Farm boys got accustomed to lugging heavy hay bales and large buckets of feed around, so you could always tell a seasoned farmer by his over-sized shoulders and knuckles that dragged along the ground. This isn't entirely true, of course, but that visualization was possibly one that helped me later in life with a decision to leave the farm and join the Navy! There was something about travelling the world that seemed infinitely more exciting than feeding farm animals. I am now envious of the modern farm operations that have all that heavy handwork mechanized. Perhaps it was a good thing that I didn't know as I was growing up, how efficient and easy a mechanized operation could be. I am quite certain that I would have traded my own baby sister for a real front-end loader to clean the manure out of the barn rather than with the shovel and wheelbarrow I was so familiar with.

Lubricating oil came in five-gallon pails with sturdy handles, which, when emptied and the lid was removed, became handy tote buckets. These pails were used to carry grain to the animals, slop and chop to the pigs, and water to the cows in winter when ice covered the pond. As a little duffer, I would drag a partially filled pail along, grunting and complaining while trying to keep it from falling over. As I grew older and stronger, I could drag two partially filled pails until I was tall enough to lift them clear of the ground. The one single factor that prevented these chores from being pure drudgery was the fact that we were a family business and each member of the family benefited from the profits and rewards.

On winter days, someone had to go down on the dugout and hack out a fresh water hole through the ice. Three or four inches of ice would have accumulated in yesterday's water hole overnight, which took a lot of chipping to make the opening large enough to dip a pail into. Naturally, as winter progressed, the water became more and more black and stagnant due to a lack of oxygen under the ice. As spring grew near, large ugly beetles would come flying out into the sunlight when the hole was opened. Those bugs had a wingspan of about two inches or more and gave me the creeps. When the ice was removed, I would dive for cover until these monstrous bugs had all escaped. Had they known that the winter air temperature would quickly freeze them solid, I think they might have remained in the dark warmth of the dugout.

Cougar cat

Ingimar, our big tomcat, would often sit poised on the roof of the porch or in the barn loft, patiently waiting for some unsuspecting human soul to emerge. As you would pause to secure the door, this massive cat would carefully aim, and then leap onto your back, expecting a soft ride to or from the barn. For those of us who were familiar with his tactics, this was routine, but for an unsuspecting visitor, he could strike sudden terror. More than once, with a terrified screech, this big tomcat went flying into a snow bank after a pinpoint landing on the back of a visiting man. The real trick for us was to remain upright with milk pails in hand, when this would-be cougar would launch from the barn loft onto our shoulders. Ingimar, aptly named after Ingimar Johansson, the world champion heavy weight boxer of the day, left all of his feline siblings meowing in the dust as he grew into this formidable farm pet.

One particular day, Ingimar was riding on my shoulder as I carried two full five-gallon pails of water up the dugout bank to the cows. (Do your math, now, each gallon of water weighs 10 pounds.) Because of water leaking from the pails, the ice steps that I had cut to climb the bank became increasingly more dangerous with each trip to the water trough. Finally, with full water pails in my hands, my foot slipped off the top step and everything went airborne. Down we went, water pails, Ingimar and me, screaming back out onto the ice! My cat let out a shriek as I hollered, "INGIMAR, LET GO!" In his desperation to save himself from pending disaster, and grasping madly for his footing, ten-pound Ingimar had hooked a claw deep into my ear. He stayed attached all the way to the bottom and then left me bawling on the ice in a pool of blood as he scrambled up on the nearby fence. It is times like this that one feels justified in trying out one or two of Father's favourite curse words, though I cannot recall that it helped any. The pain was excruciating, but the lesson was sound. I was more careful after that to preserve good footing, and no longer allowed my cat to ride on my shoulder at chore time.

As with the dogs, our farm cats were essential members of the *crew*. No farm is complete without a guard dog to warn of impending danger, or a cat to keep the rodent population at bay. So it was, that, our home was graced with the company of many generations of four-footed family members. There was many a winter when batches of kittens were born behind the woodstove, and countless times that both cats and dogs shared the foot of my bed at night.

Our family, as well as our farm animals, all seemed to get along without fighting. The family dog curled up with a sleeping cat against him, or turkeys and chickens could be found sleeping with the pigs. This was a sign of the ambient peacefulness that permeated those quiet days in the country. Sometimes, however, our animals, in their attempt to stay near us, found themselves in trouble because of it.

Dad and I drove to town after a heavy rain, one summer day. The road was very wet, so the truck was caked with mud by the time we arrived. After doing a little shopping, we paused briefly at the post office for the mail. While we were speaking with the postmaster, someone noticed this unusual shape on the open springs by the wheel of our truck. Dad said it looked like a big old root that had become caught up in the springs. He took two long strides over and pulled it out, only to find that the *muddy root* was soft and long and very frightened. Poor Ingimar had been sitting there on the truck spring when we started out from home, and being afraid of the large spinning tire beside him, had clung on for five, fearsome, bumpy miles. We peeled the mud off and took him back home, with him purring loudly in the warm cab of the truck.

Laddy, the faithful

Our family dogs changed from decade to decade. From the early years with Buster, we had several good faithful friends of man. However, living on the edge of the wilderness soon weeds out the *dogs from the pups*, so to speak. If a dog wasn't born with wilderness savvy, it usually didn't last long. Sadly, we lost a few farm dogs to fights with coyotes and porcupines. I felt

85

sorry for some of our dogs that came home from an encounter with a porcupine. Dad would have to pull the long, sharp quills out of the dog's mouth with pliers, while the dogs winced in pain.

My black and white Collie, whose name was Laddy, was especially clever and keen to protect us from harm. Laddy would follow me everywhere as I explored the creek banks and the farm, and occasionally warned me of an unnoticed bear nearby. He would help to pull me up the creek banks, and in winter would pull me along on homemade skis. Dad built a wooden sled with metal edged runners and a clever harness out of a flat drive belt from the old threshing machine. Laddy was so eager to pull, that whenever we came outside in the winter, he would voluntarily climb into the harness and stand there in the snow, happily wagging his tail. This dog was so duty oriented that even when his feet became sore and bleeding from the sharp road ice, he would still climb into his harness and beg to pull me around. Because Laddy was so keen, Father made him a set of leather moccasins out of old work gloves that would protect his feet and prevent further damage.

For years, the school division had an inconceivable rule that allowed the school bus only a quarter of a mile off of the main road for pickup. For so many of us, this would mean that we were left up to our own resources to get the rest of the way home. For me, it meant a mile of walking, or if the weather was poor, I might get a ride in the truck. Happily, during nice weather, there was much for a young lad to explore and study along the way to or from the bus.

The cold of winter, however, was not the time to dally around, because if one did not keep moving vigorously, you could soon lose the feeling in your hands or feet. Here is where faithful Laddy came to my aid many a snowy winter day. All suited up in his harness, he would dutifully pull me a mile down the road on the sled to catch the bus. I would then turn the sled around for him and send him home again. Laddy was again a welcome sight when I got off the bus. Some days, I was unable to see very far in the swirling snow, but here would come my faithful old friend, ploughing through the fresh snow with the sled behind to give me a ride home. Mom would listen for the sound of the bus out along the correction line road before putting Laddy in the harness with instructions to fetch me from the bus. My old friend taught me a valuable lesson about being faithful and true, even in the face of danger and discomfort.

He was my constant companion for many more years, but as a young teenager, I had to finally put Laddy to rest. He was old and suffering from arthritis with large, painful growths on his body, so my father said that it was not fair to allow Laddy to suffer so much just to have his company. He said the compassionate thing to do was to end his pain and that he hoped I would understand. That was a hard lesson in understanding not to be selfish. Many years have slipped by since that day, but I still miss my faithful old friend, and I think of him each year when the snow begins to fall.

A "higher" education

Throughout my boyhood, I lived in a kind of peaceful dream world when I was out alone in the forest. The silence of the forest and the presence of the wildlife were fascinating to me, and kept drawing me back to their domain. I wonder now how many of my father's tools disappeared along the creek banks on days when I would *borrow* them for little building projects somewhere out there.

I was gifted with a great imagination, which, when encouraged by nature's wild land, entertained me for many years. There were so many other boys that I knew who sat playing games, or in later years watched television. But, for me, the great outdoors was all the entertainment I needed. To this very day, I look to the hills to satiate that need to escape the noise of society. As often as possible, I climb down along some lonely stream to enjoy the quiet tranquility of nature.

Nature taught me how to listen, to move slowly and carefully when trouble is near. It taught me an appreciation for a beauty that is not man made, but can only be found in what humans have not spoiled.

Countless hours of my time were spent studying industrious beaver as they built their lodges or dams, watching birds build their nests or examining coyote or bear dens. I learned so much from the natural order of the wild and found it a peaceful contrast to what I find prevalent in man's world.

At times, bull moose or buck deer would compete with one another of his species for *family status*, but when the negotiations were complete, they never returned to attack out of vengeance or hate, as man does. A male animal would naturally choose a healthy female to begin a family with, and go off to raise their young in the quiet of the forest. They never competed with each other for anything but the right to be a valued member of their society.

I see this order as nature's "established normal." I have yet to find a drunken animal lying in the gutter, or a drug-crazed, wild creature looking for some pleasure beyond what they enjoy in the wilderness. Perhaps, as humans, we believe that we have need of these destructive pleasures, simply because we have all but destroyed the wonderful peace and beauty that was ours to enjoy in the backwoods...I don't know. I wonder how many people are aware of that beautiful, peaceful world just beyond the pavement?

Contrary to *somebody's* tale, there has actually never been a desire in me to leave society and disappear into the hinterland forever, although momentary departures from our noisy world are most agreeable.

Living by the principles that I learned on the homestead and out in the wild, have for me, never been a disappointment. Man can learn a great deal by following the normal pattern of life displayed in nature.

There are often significant experiences in a person's life that serve to change their worldview, their philosophy or their purpose in life. As for me...

My homestead upbringing made me so very thankful to have been a farm boy.

Travelling the world and experiencing our spectacular country from coast to coast made me proud to be a Canadian and taught me an appreciation for cultural differences.

The Royal Canadian Navy taught me personal discipline and greatly increased my self-esteem.

My children give me great purpose to live and an even greater appreciation for life.

But, the beauty of nature, as we find it vibrant in the wilderness, nurtured me and formed me as a passionate outdoorsman, a lover of peace and forever a devoted "Child of the Land."

Chapter
Four

My life
as Tarzan

Baby creatures
big and small

As an energetic preschooler, I most often tagged along behind my Mom or Dad out on the farm somewhere. While Dad was working out in the field on the John Deere tractor, I helped Mom take care of the house and garden. She would feed the calves, the little pigs, the chickens and geese, while our family dog Buster and I would follow along making friends with everybody. We had an inexhaustible supply of pet chickens, pet geese, pet calves and sometimes, little *oinkers.*

One day, my father bought a purebred Yorkshire piglet that, as I recall, was the cutest creature in the universe. (That was before girls.) For its protection, Mom and Dad allowed this little pig to share its first few weeks of life with us in the warmth of the house.

Next to my dog, this little pig became my best friend for a good year or so before he went off into the world. His name was Elmer and would come when called, and much to my dog's embarrassment, was even obedient. Although Elmer was a pig, he was perfectly house-trained and clean, and would scratch at the door to be let out when duty called. When hungry, he would again scratch at the cupboard for food. As Elmer grew, he was moved back to the barnyard but still preferred to follow me around and would rather be playing up at the house. In time, Elmer and I enjoyed some serious exploration together and with Buster the dog along, we roamed far afield, out across the farm.
A year or so later, when Elmer was grown and had been sold, my dad and I were in the area of his new

home and stopped in to see how he was fairing. Ben Gaboury was his new owner, and when we asked him how Elmer was getting along with the other pigs and animals, Ben laughed and said, "Watch this!" From the fence, he called, "Elmer! Here, Elmer!" Within seconds, there was a stir amongst the field full of pigs, and here came Elmer, pushing his way through the crowd, coming right up to me, putting his front feet up on my jacket. It was hard to leave him again, but my Dad used that moment to teach me a lesson about economics, (which still didn't seem like a decent reason to separate good friends).

When I was about seven or so, we raised another little orphan cutie with a flat nose and the most endearing personality. I named her Olivia after the girl I was sweet on in school. She was equally as much fun as Elmer, and we spent many happy hours playing together.

One day, she inadvertently taught me a valuable lesson about women that I shall never forget. In my enthusiasm, I innocently announced in school one day that I owned this pet pig, which I had affectionately named after Olivia. I looked right at Olivia, expecting her to be overjoyed with the association, but she dashed from the room and wouldn't talk to me again that whole year. Well, it beats me! I thought it was a great connection. I mean this was a *very cute* little pig!

Spring was a great time to make new friends on the farm. As a small boy, there were numerous friendships made with little baby calves. Those clumsy little four legged creatures would follow you along, chewing your coat or sucking on your fingers as though you were their own mother. If they could not get a taste of milk, however, they would give you a mighty bunt, hoping for a squirt of nourishment. Now when you're only a little tyke, a bunt like that would often leave you flat on your pants in the barnyard muck.

My duty was to go around and check all the calves each time I was in the barnyard. The job was to check them all for runny bums, (delightful!) which was an indication that they were not feeling well. Fortunately, their upset tummies could be quickly cured by a spoonful of Doctor Bell's, a versatile medicine that seemed to be used for many animal ailments. It was, however, always a trick to administer the medicine to these wiggly creatures without spilling it, so one had to be persistent and strong.

All baby creatures like to chew on things, so another of my duties when in the barnyard, was to watch for remnants of baler twine in the mouths of the little calves. When hay bales were opened, the strings were stashed on fence posts to keep them out of the feed. The calves would often suck on the ends of the loops of baler twine hanging down, and on occasion, get one loose and swallow it! These little animals have no less than five stomachs, so a long, heavy string like this can become lodged for a very long time. Removing the twine takes a slow but steady pull, while the calf gags and gulps and tries to swallow it again.

The cows were to be milked for profit, so at some point in their early lives, the baby calves had to leave their mother and receive a measured amount of milk by pail. If she was carefully managed, a cow could produce enough milk for both her calf and for sale. This milk was then separated so that we could sell the cream.

When the calves and the cows were separated for this purpose, it was a noisy and stressful time for the herd, with the babies calling for moms and the cows calling for the youngsters. To quiet all the bawling, we had to quickly teach the baby calves to drink milk from a bucket, which always proved to be an entertaining process. They instinctively reach upward to suck from a warm, controlled source, so presenting them with a cold bucket of milk below their noses would obviously incite some confusion. It was so pathetic to watch those poor hungry little faces blowing bubbles in the milk pail without ever swallowing a drop. Often, they would bunt the bucket in frustration, sending us over backward in a shower of fresh milk.

Eventually, by wetting our fingers in the milk and inserting them into the baby's mouth, we could slowly lower its head and rough, slobbery, little tongue back into the milk again. After several attempts, these hungry little guys would overcome the snorting, sneezing and gurgling to blissfully slurp up the liquid from the bottom of the pail. As kids, we soon learned not to dally around once the pail was empty. One moment too long, and you could well be wearing the bucket yourself, as a 75-pound baby can be very assertive when the milk runs out!

Nowadays, parents will often devise make-work projects for their children to keep them out of idleness, but many years ago on the homestead, there was no need for such projects. There was more than enough work to do for the whole family. I did wonder about the validity of jobs such as shovelling manure or snow. I mean, isn't there supposed to be a machine to do that stuff?

One year, as an early teen, I looked after our neighbour's pigs for a few weeks in the winter. Before he left on his trip, Mr. Wenger had shown me that the first job each day was to remove the stinking, sloppy manure from inside the barn. (Have you ever smelled pig manure? I would not recommend it!) This entailed the use of a flat shovel to heave the runny muck through a one-foot square hole in the wall at about eye level. I was a good shot, but learned to keep one eye closed in case of splash back! When I came back home, my mom always signalled me to disrobe out in the porch to get rid of my pig clothes. Now I ask you, who in their right mind would design such a manure removal system? I suppose that is why they hire kids for such a job ... kids can't complain (no one seems to listen anyway), and thankfully they are washable.

In pursuit of a higher calling

While growing up, my all time favourite job was fetching the cows for milking. This entailed a long walk down through the creek banks and often to the far end of the farm. These natural, wild lands with the creek flowing through it had become my paradise, and there, as an imaginative boy, I could be Robinson Crusoe, Robin Hood or even Tarzan. Thus, my daily walk to fetch the cows for milking sometimes took longer than it should have, and likely made my mother worry.

The cartoons and comic books of the day further stimulated my imagination, and Tarzan was a real hero with a real purpose in life that fascinated me. So it was, that I spent countless hours on the banks of the Fox Creek and the adjoining forest, pretending that I was that famous jungle hero.

96

My life as Tarzan

Tarzan possessed an amazing ability to speak to the animals and somehow commanded them to join him in his worthy endeavours. I have to admit, however, the only animals I was ever able to command with any degree of success were the cows that I was sent to bring home for milking each night.

When I was a youngster, I had seemingly unlimited time alone with my thoughts and imagination in the great outdoors. This led me into many battles with imaginary enemies, wildly racing up secret ravines or climbing down over steep cliffs to rescue some poor, helpless child. There seemed to be a great need in my life to pursue a higher calling, and in my imagination, the life I spent as Tarzan gave me that imaginative practice. For many hours, I lay hidden, spying on the activity of wild beaver that were working on their dams or lodges, or watching a doe with a spring fawn, grazing along the edge of a field of new hay. I was a rescuer with a solemn, imaginary duty to liberate and protect.

I wasn't aware of it at the time, of course, but this would be valuable preparation for the responsibilities I would face in the future. Responsibilities such as military service for my country, a Park Ranger accountable for conservation and the safety of my park and visitors, or a father nurturing and protecting my children. As a paramedic helping the injured or as a minister helping the homeless, these romantic, childhood days on the homestead would develop in me a mindset for the future.

Freedom defined

I have since heard of many a young man who learned a great deal about himself and his world just by playing in a vacant lot on the edge of town or in someone's nearby field. As for me, I had the greatest of all places to explore and learn. If my father's 480 acres were not enough, as I grew older I had free run of thousands of acres of neighbouring fields and forest as far as my legs could carry me.

So, explore I did, and once every stream and meadow was discovered on the homestead, I expanded my wanderings into new and unknown territory. Today, freedom still defines itself in me as the ability to explore the lakes and streams of some nearby park or mountainous wild land. I can readily appreciate the famous poet Robert Service, as he aptly describes being called to those wonderful, lonely places. Out there, away from all of man's noisy contrivances, one is able to find an abiding joy in the peacefulness of nature.

Robert Service also penned a popular poem called, "The Land That God Forgot." On occasion, we experienced 45 or 50 degree below-zero winter days that would in fact make you think that He had indeed forgotten this land! Possibly, He may have just had trouble with the global heating system. At any rate, periodic cold snaps occasionally confined us indoors.

As I grew older, the call of the wild was becoming noticeably stronger, and by the age of ten, I took advantage of every opportunity to be out in the wilderness.

My life as Tarzan

I am certain my folks and my friends never quite understood me at times when the weather was at its very worst. There was something intriguing about the outdoors that called to me, something I cannot explain. At times like this, I would often suit up and strike out into the cold. Mother made me a set of puttees, which are long, narrow strips of cloth with which I could wrap my legs from my knees to my boots. These simple puttees kept the snow out and the heat in. Indian moccasins were my favourite winter footwear and were quite warm when worn inside my rubber overshoes. This combination allowed me to remain out in the cold and storm for hours on end before reluctantly returning from the quiet of the wild to the warmth of our home.

Every season had its special attractions, but strangely, winter storms drew me to their snowy swirl like a warrior's challenge. Mother always made certain that I had a warm, winter jacket and a woolly sweater to keep me from freezing. The air would be wholesomely fresh with a smell of supreme cleanliness, as I tightened my storm hood around my face. For some reason, it gave me a certain thrill to just fade into the blowing snow and disappear among the trees. If one was very quiet, a deer or a cow moose could be found taking shelter in the densest part of the forest, waiting for the storm to end. There were delightful times that I burrowed down in the snow in a wind-sheltered part of the forest and sat stock still for an hour. It doesn't take long before you become part of the landscape, with the snow covering all trace of your being there. Strangely, this brings about a feeling of absolute freedom.

As winter progressed, travel became more and more difficult. Some years, snow accumulations in northern Alberta reached three or four feet deep, making foot travel very strenuous. When I was about twelve, I asked for a pair of snowshoes for Christmas so I could get around better in all that white powder. My parents purchased a good quality set, which was to become the handiest gift I had ever received. What wonderful freedom these snowshoes gave me to explore further into the winter wonderland. My poor old dog was sad to be left behind, because now I was able to travel in snow far too deep for him to follow. Because of their shape, snowshoes are much more useful in the bush than skis, with the opposite being true when travelling out on an open field.

On a peaceful Saturday morning, while checking my trap line, I emerged from the forest to cross a small meadow. It had been snowing all night, so there were six inches of fresh powder covering the old snow pack. As I tramped unaware out to the centre of this quiet paddock, I received the fright of my life. Suddenly, the whole landscape seemed to explode in a flurry of snow and noise that gave me the sensation of falling into the centre of the earth! In fear, I crouched down, not understanding what was happening. To my astonishment, I had walked into the middle of a whole flock of wild grouse that, when disturbed, had erupted from under the snow where they had been sleeping. It took several minutes before I could regain my composure and continue on my trek.

A young trapper

Although I despised trapping as a way of making money, I continued with my line for a few years. The one great attraction was the joy of being out in the quiet wilderness, far from home. This enterprise also earned me a few dollars of spending money and a degree of independence. It was the undersized weasel skins that were my main problem. The Hudson's Bay Raw Fur department in Grande Prairie would pay only a glass of draft beer for these little females. Of course, being only twelve years old at the time, I had to give up some of my earnings to my father!

By the middle of winter, we would often get very tired of eating moose meat and longed for a change of diet. The Native people from Sturgeon Lake would help us out in this respect, and occasionally bring to town a whole truckload of frozen whitefish. Since the outside temperature was colder than your normal deep freeze, they simply marketed these fish from the back of an open pickup truck. People could then come by and dig through the catch to choose which ones they wanted. The fish were sold for a dollar each, and despite the many bones, they were a tasty delight.

Life on the homestead was so very different than life in your average city suburb. In the city, one might suffer a home invasion from human thieves or have trouble with a neighbour's dog, but seldom will your livelihood be threatened or your food supply robbed. On the farm, however, our livestock had to be constantly watched and protected from hungry, wild animals prowling nearby.

Hunting bear

One wet spring, we had just such an unwanted visitor to the pigpen, and sadly, one of our little weaner pigs disappeared. Confirming our worst fears, we found black bear tracks in the area and were able to follow them back to the bear's den. At that time, we only had a small calibre gun on hand, which was insufficient to address a problem of that size. So, when Dad went to town that week, he solicited the help of some big fellows with big guns. I remember our tractor arriving back home making deep tracks in the spring mud, carrying Father and two other men on board. The men accepted a coffee and warmed up a bit before venturing out to see if they could accost Mr. Bear. Dad showed them where the den was situated and joined the mighty hunters as they approached with guns at the ready.

All was quiet except for the whisper of a spring breeze. They discussed their plan in low voices and then began firing into the ground to scare the animal out. Not a stir was noticed. One fellow said, "Maybe he's not home right now. Cover me, and I will crawl down and look into the den." The other men stood poised, ready to shoot, while this man lay quietly down on his belly and peered into the dark cavern. All of a sudden he yelled, "OH, MAN! (As well as some other unmentionable adjectives.) You're darn right there is a bear in there!" as he leaped away, clambering for his rifle. Still shaking, he stood way back, exclaiming that he had looked in and almost touched noses with the bear as it was coming out!

The three *brave* men then stood positioned over the entrance of the den, discussing what they should do. "We should at least give him a running chance," one said, and they all agreed to let the animal leave the den before shooting it. The problem was, that the den had been dug by a smaller bear some years earlier, and this larger one was having quite a struggle trying to get his chubby body back out of the hole again. The men waited, the bear squirmed, and then ... Blam! A rifle report echoed across the valley. "Ok, who's the wise guy?" Father asked. The man with the smoking gun grinned in his embarrassment. "Sorry, I guess I was a little jumpy."

Our poor pig thief never did get a running chance. He scarcely got his head out before someone dispatched him to bear heaven. Women and children were then allowed out of the house, having been given the *all-clear* signal. The men pulled the bear the rest of the way out of the hole and were posing victoriously for photographs, when Mom, my sister and I arrived. Up to that moment, I had believed that we were banned to the house to be protected from a marauding bear, but now it was clear that our greatest danger was from these trigger-happy hunters. Truly, we needed help in this instance to rid ourselves of this dangerous animal, but my father felt badly and never again asked for help to deal with such a problem.

Gentle at heart

As I grew, I became more useful as a farm hand. However, much to my father's disappointment, there were some areas of farm work that I abhorred. Working the land with machines and understanding the business of agriculture became increasingly interesting to me, but alas, there were certain aspects in the handling of the animals that I never could get used to.

This realization began when I was barely three years old. Dad and Mr. Newland were butchering a pig to divide between the families to supplement our food supply. Neither of those seasoned farmers cringed at the process of wrestling that poor, squealing pig over to the site and cutting its throat. They had skillfully erected a tripod of poles on which to suspend the animal, and below it was a barrel of boiling water, waiting to scald the creature after it was dead. This would loosen the bristly hair so that it could be easily removed, leaving the skin clean and ready for butchering. With tears in my eyes, I stood way back and plugged my ears at the sound of that screaming animal. I finally could stand it no longer and erupted in a flurry of indistinguishable words while throwing a barrage of sticks and mud lumps at the men. I don't recall my dad being especially understanding at the time, but I took my stand, and that was the beginning of my awareness of who I really was.

There has never been a time when I was comfortable with that part of farming. Whether it was killing chickens for the frying pan, dehorning cattle or castrating the young bulls, I never got used to it and to this day, I hate the thought of hurting one of God's living creatures. This was, however, one of farming's necessary jobs, and to prosper in that business is to learn to do the work. I am just thankful that my dad did not run cattle on the community pasture, and therefore, we did not have to brand the poor creatures.

Blueberry Mountain

A few times a year, we packed the car and drove west to spend the day with our cousins at Blueberry Mountain. This was my Uncle Bob and Aunt Arletta's farm, where they were struggling to raise seven hungry children. Blueberry Mountain, though not much of a mountain, was an area of exquisite beauty and a picture of nature's perfection. When summer colours were splashed across the landscape, the *mountain* appeared to me as some celestial park, painted by a great artist. The Hampton family lived in their squared log house up on a hill so that one could look out across the valley and enjoy the view for virtually twenty to thirty miles. The fields were rimmed with rows of lush poplar trees, and there were clumps of

105

bushes scattered here and there across the park-like pastureland. Uncle Bob's cattle grazed lazily in the meadows and enjoyed the shade of tall trees by the watering pond at the end of the quarter section.

When visiting our cousins, we would race through the puddles, across the pasture and through the bush, playing games of Cowboys-and-Indians or Hide-and-Seek. We often played out there "until the cows came home" as the saying goes, when we would find our way back to the house, tired and hungry.

The supper table in the Hampton home was a flurry of chatter and excitement, with everyone diving for moose burger and hot veggies. With all of my cousins around, I have enjoyed many a wholesome meal at that table. After supper, the screen door would swing and slam, and the chatter of happy children's voices could once again be heard all over the farm. Some would be raiding the garden, while some might be down on the pier at the pond. Usually, the boys continued playing Cowboys-and-Indians, often engaged in a great shoot-out from the fortress of the icehouse. The family dog was never quite sure which side to favour, so repeatedly stood dumbly beside the one who was attempting to hide in the bushes!

The Hampton boys were well schooled by their father and were all proficient hunters. Thus, I repeatedly lost to their expertise while target shooting. Our BB guns and pellet guns were hot some days at the little rifle range we would set up. The danger was in keeping younger kids from dashing through the firing line. Once, in the heat of a dart-throwing contest, someone did dash in front of the target area and caught a dart in the side of his head!

Over the years, our most favourite pastime was sitting around the kitchen table and listening to our fathers recall their adventures. Girls and boys alike would sit spellbound, glued to the tales of the storyteller.

Countless summer days were spent swimming and exploring around Moonshine Lake Park where we would meet the Hamptons for picnics. My Uncle Bob became caretaker of the park when it was still in its early stages of development. As the years went by, many thousands of people enjoyed this area for family recreation, while the park grew into the popular destination it is today. My mother's standard picnic lunch would be cold, fried chicken and potato salad with gallons of Kool-Aid for the children to guzzle. What a contrast for my parents, sitting there by the lake watching their children play while remembering their first cold winter, tenting at the old sawmill on this very site. Today, as though a family tradition, my cousin Rob continues as Maintenance and Operations Manager of this same park that his father once managed.

Some of the Hampton family are still on the Mountain today and remain a tribute to the strength and dedication of their parents. Summer days were valuable workdays in the business of agriculture. Legume and cereal crops alike were dependent upon moisture and hot sun for success, so we had to tend to our crops when the weather was good. Good weather also provides a window of opportunity for building projects or for the necessary repairs of equipment and facilities on the farm. When weekends arrived, however, my sister and I would plead and whine to our parents for a chance to visit the river or for a day at the lake. If, by chance, we were caught up with the farm work and the sun was hot, our parents would sometimes drive the ten miles to a little municipal park along the Peace River. Here, we were near the water and I would be in my glory.

Parks are for families

Mother especially enjoyed the little picturesque park by the Peace River, which is now called Kieyho Park. Being a Saskatchewan kid and growing up on a farm where there was an abundance of rocks, she felt right at home along the rocky riverbed. Since there were virtually no rocks in the soil of our farm, Mom would collect these gems from anywhere that she could find them, and eventually, she developed a large rock garden out of her collected treasures. Once, I remember Mother and Father going for a long walk upstream along the Peace River while my sister Sylvia and I played happily in the sand along the bank for what seemed like hours. Finally, late in the evening, we could see them making their way slowly back along the river shore. Mom had an armful of *precious* little rocks, and poor old Dad was struggling along with an enormous piece of flat shale. He did not seem to be impressed with his new role of "beast of burden," and the conversation was noticeably quiet on the drive home!

Once or twice each summer, we would drive the forty dusty miles to Winagami Lake where a small, informal park was being developed. Here, the waves were high, the air was full of sea birds and spray the way I envisioned the ocean might be. My parents and little sister would spend the day relaxing in the shade of the tall poplars while I roamed the beach and spent countless hours in the water. For some unknown reason, there was a strange draw to these bodies of water that I was unable to resist. These sultry, warm days of summer by the lake were great family times and highlights in our lives. Today, Winagami Lake has developed into a provincial park and a very popular tourist destination.

It appears that a appreciation of nature runs in the family and it is interesting to note that many years later, my own children would be interested in camping, skiing and hiking. Three of my four daughters would experience park picnics and a campout by the time they were a few weeks old; the exception being Julie Anne who was born while we were working and living in the serenity of Manning Provincial Park in British Columbia. Now, years later, they may be found happily exploring local parks or camping along some picturesque waterway at every available opportunity.

I now readily understand why my hero Tarzan left an educated existence in high society for the solitude of the jungle, even if he was only a cartoon character.

Chapter
Five

Developing
a latent gift

Defining my interests

Every moving machine seems to hold a boy's interest, and being a country boy, I learned at an early age to operate all the machinery on the farm. Consequently, it was difficult to pay attention in a schoolroom when farm tractors or trucks were working nearby or when an aircraft flew overhead. As the son of an Engineer, I was about to learn what it means to be born with latent interests.

The fascination with machines was stimulated in me from the time I learned to crawl. My inventor/builder/toy-maker-father first carved a solid, wooden airplane with a spinning propeller, which was presented to me before I could walk. My folks also gave me a toy John Deere tractor with an implement to pull, like the big one that Father drove. Before I could walk, I would *help* Mother in the garden, using my little toy farm equipment. Out on the farm fields, we could hear the real John Deere tractor with its two-cylinder engine, going "pop, pop, pop." Many a day, I *worked* at home in the garden or the flowerbed, mimicking that sound with my toy tractor.

By my fourth birthday, there was a larger, more interesting box for me under the Christmas tree. Upon shredding the package, a most extraordinary toy emerged. Through the long winter evenings, my dad had laboured to build an intricate, working model of his Massey-Harris combine for me. This incredible toy was powered by a Big Ben clock motor, which could be wound up through a keyhole in one wheel. My fabulous, new toy would rumble along the floor on its homemade tires like the real machine. It had rubber belts that ran the straw spreader at the rear, as well as the rotating reel up front. This little model was intricately painted in authentic Massey-Harris colours of red and yellow and proudly displayed the name *Hassey-Marris* on the side of the grain hopper. I was so proud of that toy that for a long time it went with me everywhere.

Over the years, there were many mechanical toys and road building models that influenced me, but my all-time favourite toy when confined to the house, was an elaborate, factory made Meccano Set. This ingenious set was made up of small sections of metal with pre-drilled holes for the tiny bolts to fasten to. It came complete with wheels, axles, pulleys and cranks, and just like my father's big shop outside, it was supplied with wrenches and other miniature tools for long hours of imaginative fun.

This particular skill-building toy would undoubtedly have the largest impact on my early mechanical development, and the years of designing and building which would follow. No doubt one can still find tiny nuts and bolts hiding in the cracks of that old cabin floor. I learned to build tractors, trucks and elaborate cranes out of my Meccano Set, as well as airplanes and buildings. As I grew older and stronger, I slowly graduated to full size building material found around the homestead and the larger tools in my father's toolbox.

For a mechanically minded young man like myself, the best part of living on the farm was, of course, the selection of motors and machines that were our basic business tools. Because these machines were working in dirt and water out on the land, they suffered heavy wear resulting in the constant threat of a breakdown. At an early age, I learned to go equipped with the necessary tools and supplies to repair any problem I might encounter. (The exception might be when one crashes into the fence with the tractor, pulling thirty feet of harrows on an outside turn at the end of the field!] A whole shop full of tools was required to adequately repair that damage! This, of course, never happens unless the said tractor operator happens to be daydreaming he is Tarzan chasing Jane through the jungle, but we won't talk about that!

Age two, heavy equipment training

My training in heavy equipment operation began at the age of two, standing on Dad's lap to steer the tractor. By age four, my legs still were not long enough to reach the distant pedals, so I stood on the seat to steer the snorting old John Deere. Dad would instruct me to aim at some distant object to keep the tractor going straight, while he walked along and threw large roots and sticks up on the stone boat (a kind of land raft) behind. At the end of the field, he would precariously clamber up the tow chain from the stone boat to the tractor in time to help me turn the beast before we ran out of field.

I once ran over a porcupine with the tractor and it scurried under the stone boat. I began yelling and jumping up and down on the seat, but of course could not reach any of the controls that would stop the machine! That was the day that I graduated from the *how to operate the throttle* class. We thankfully had much more control from that time on.

114

Why farm kids RULE!

The main reason that farm kids grew up so quickly handling horses, bulls and cows, and operating every piece of equipment we owned, was that few families had the ready cash to hire an adult to help out with the work. Some of us kids were driving the grain truck at harvest time as early as 10 or 12 years old, and certainly operating a simple farm tractor much earlier than that. It was exposure to these experiences that developed my mechanical aptitude and a keen interest in moving machines that would span a lifetime.

Throughout the years, such fond memories were created, like driving the International grain truck when I could only peer between the top of the steering wheel and the dash. By the time I was twelve or thirteen, Dad would have me manoeuvre alongside the moving combine so that the grain could be augured (pumped) from the harvester into the truck while we were still on the move. When the truck was full, Dad would give a wave from the combine and continue on down the field. My job would be to drive the heavily loaded truck out of the field and five miles into town to the grain elevator. Here, I would dump the load, and the elevator agent would record the grade and amount to be credited to our account. Harvest, and indeed most of the farming business, was a family affair. The *whole* family became actively involved in the busy schedule of each farming season. Mother, of course, was our number one *man* next to Dad, and my sister and I always had some job to do to support the operation.

I did not know it at the time, but so many valuable lessons learned on the farm would hold me in good stead for years to come. The wide scope of education we received as farm kids gave most of us a great start in every area of life.

My dad, like most farm dads, had a marvellous workshop and inventory of steel and wood for fabrication. His workshop was complete with mechanic's tools, woodworking tools and a full supply of nuts, bolts and everything else needed for building. When I was not out exploring, this became my playground, and also shaped my thinking in many ways. When a young mind is left to design and build, and all of the necessary equipment and materials are available, there are sure to be many hours of entertainment ahead.

Lumber, in those early years did not come from the city lumberyard or hardware store, because these stores were simply too far away. There often was, however, someone working in the country with a sawmill that would cut the lumber needed for any building project. For country kids, the best part of this lumber making venture was that after the mill had moved on to another building project, it left behind a large pile of slabs. Slabs are the round part of the outside of each tree which often still had the bark attached. These slabs made great firewood, fencing material and cheap, building material for young boys with imaginative building projects. With even a small amount of creativity, spruce slabs could become cabins, cowboys' corrals or even futuristic space vessels. This, of course, all depended upon Father's ready supply of tools and nails.

Developing a latent gift

Fortunately, my dad recognized the importance of keeping me supplied with all the building necessities. (Doubtless, this also kept me out of his busy way, thus evading my unquenchable stream of questions.) I can still see poor old Dad lying on his back, working on some piece of farm equipment and unable to escape my constant chatter. It was not difficult, though, to determine when he was tired of answering me. At that point in time, his response to every question became, "Well, that is just to make little boys ask questions."

Then, it was time to go and pester my unsuspecting mother while she pulled weeds in the garden. Mom was a fantastic lady. She was a bundle of perpetual movement from the time her feet hit the cold floor in the morning until the lights went out at night. I have seen few women in my life that could even begin to handle the workload that my mother could. She was a proficient farm manager, planner, gardener, mother and accomplished chef.

As I bombarded her with questions about life on this planet, she never slowed her pace or stopped her work, but she also never discouraged me from asking questions. Absorbing every bit of knowledge from her mind that I could in those formative years gave us a great deal of time together. There was not a day in my childhood that I could not come to Mom with all the deep questions of life, which she was happy to answer to the best of her ability. She was always quick to exert her opinions as well, which stimulated some relative debate.

Dad was still the ready source of engineering knowledge that I needed to complete many of my building projects. Luckily, projects like this were also something that interested him enough to tolerate my many questions.

Father's innovative leadership

When we first moved our cabin to the new yard site, Dad designed and built a small generator to provide electricity for our house. This was marvellous to my mom and me, as we no longer had to light the house with the gas lantern. We saw it as such a modern convenience, that we ignored the loud chugging of the one-lunger gas-engine that powered the generator outside. Although the lights would flicker up and down with each stroke of that old engine, we still had visitors come from all around the country to marvel at Dad's homemade electrical system. That was one of the many inventions that he designed and built to ease the rough life on the Project in those days and that influenced my understanding of mechanics.

Store-bought rope was expensive, so when we needed rope, we made our own. Again, Father built a clever device for this purpose. It was a rope maker and had a rotating handle, which could twist several lengths of binder twine together. Each string had to twist individually, as well as simultaneously wind the whole group tightly together, fabricating the rope. As such, we always had long lengths of good rope, handy for all kinds of uses.

Another of my dad's many inventions was a chicken brooder. Each spring, our annual supply of baby chicks would come in on the train, packaged in big, flat cardboard boxes full of little, round breathing holes. Out of each of the holes protruded a tiny little head, and the whole box was alive with warmth and soft peeping. These little fluffy birds had to be kept safe and warm while they grew, so Father's brooder was developed for this purpose. It looked like a tiny hotel with enough room for fifty chicks to live and grow. Since he developed this before we had electricity, a coal oil lamp was used to supply heat under the little brooder to keep these little fluff balls safe from the elements. There was also feed and water in their little straw-filled home so they could grow in warmth and comfort. As well, there was a runway where they could come and go to the outside world. This homemade incubator served us for many years, raising literally hundreds of little chickens.

Compared to the modern farms of today, our first years in agriculture were quite slow. Most of the equipment was small and some was actually designed for use behind horses. Dad preferred our little AR John Deere tractor to horses, but was always looking for ways to speed up the farm production. They say that necessity is the mother of invention, which as time went on, brought about the development of more than one innovative device.

In the early years of homesteading, Dad found a way to eliminate the need for a hired hand to operate his 10 ft. power binder that was pulled behind the tractor. A binder was a machine that preceded today's modern combine and swather. It was specifically designed to cut down a standing crop of grain and neatly package the grain in bundles, called sheaves, tied together with twine. The sheaves would then eject out the side of the binder onto the ground. This required someone to walk along and stand them up against one another into little pyramids so they would shed the rain. This was called "stooking."

To streamline the operation, Dad had fastened a long, steel rod with a universal joint from the steering column of the tractor, back to the binder. He could then sit way back and operate the binder and be able to drive the tractor at the same time, thus eliminating the need for a tractor operator. One fall day, as Dad was using this equipment, our neighbour Frank Newland said, "Hey, why don't you hook my binder on behind yours and we could work twice as fast!" Newlie's was a smaller, 7-foot-wide horse-drawn binder, and with the two machines together, they could harvest both men's crops a great deal quicker.

One sunny day, Dad was out in the field, preparing to unhitch the tractor from the binder to come home for dinner. Nick, our neighbour and good friend, came along about that time to see this ingenious piece of equipment at work. Dad showed him how it was put together and explained all the advantages. "May I try it out, Frank?" he asked. "Go ahead," said Dad. "I will walk in to eat and we will see you back at the house." Nick climbed on the binder, and with a "Pop, Pop, Pop" of the John Deere, he roared off down the field. Dad went merrily home, proud of his machine, but hungry for dinner. Some time later, Nick arrived back at the house looking rather annoyed and shaken up, and said to my dad, "Everything works great, Frank, but how do you turn the darn thing?" Dad's face paled a little as he sat back down. "Oh no," he said, "I was getting ready to disconnect when you came along, and I forgot to hook up the steering rod again!" That was the day our friend Nick nearly won an unplanned tour of the creek before he was able to stop the whole

120

machine. Nick and Dad are still friends today and laugh about the incident, but I do not recall him ever again asking to try out another one of Father's new contraptions.

On the homestead, as it has always been in the world, people were our greatest resource. Watching my parents interact with other busy homesteaders developed a valuable mindset needed for my own future. From the time I could walk, folks were always ready to help other people in need. It might be a simple sharing of wild game or help to fix a broken machine. Often, it was only the contribution of expertise that each pioneer was able to offer to his fellow neighbour. One man would be a skilled carpenter or mechanic, while another would be good at veterinary work. One might have a piece of equipment for a specialized purpose, or maybe just have the time to help you out. Men and women depended a lot on each other in the early years of the *Project*. These interactions and the experiences of kindness transformed a struggling community into a thriving family of homesteaders.

Is my Daddy gonna die?

With ongoing development in the country, there was always a requirement for an operating sawmill. When a sawmill was moved from one project to another, it usually required more than one tractor to pull it over the soft ground. Father was asked to help with a sawmill move one fateful day, when a terrible accident occurred. As the men came across a field to a road allowance, the mill got hung up in the ditch. Both tractors then spun out, leaving the whole operation suspended. About the time the men were ready to give up and go home, a neighbour with a more powerful tractor arrived and offered to help. They chained this third machine ahead of Father's, and the pull began again. All the machines pulling at full power caused one of the heavy steel chains to break, which whipped back, striking my father on the neck and knocking him off the tractor! When Mom and I arrived, Dad was lying in the dirt with blood oozing from his mouth and ears! We carefully packed him on the back of a smaller tractor and drove the two bumpy miles back home again. (Understanding the critical nature of cervical injuries now, I am amazed that the tractor ride alone did not kill him.) Mom then worriedly bundled him up and drove the next forty miles in the old truck to the hospital. He had damaged his cervical vertebrae and torn a major tendon in his neck. It was a month before I saw my dad again, and when I did, he was in a full body cast and confined to bed rest. That experience taught me that chains made of steel do not stretch, and are extremely dangerous when under great pressure. I have been careful of heavy chain loads my whole life due to that one memory.

As the years went by, our farm machines and our knowledge of mechanics expanded to meet the new challenges. More and more modern equipment replaced the original old machines, vastly speeding up the farming operations. A snowplough was fabricated to fit on our largest tractor, and hydraulics eventually replaced the old manual lift equipment. Each and every day, we were faced with mechanical problems that required troubleshooting. As a young farmer, it was a constant challenge to remember to check the many possible problem areas of each operation. Inevitably, things did go wrong and I humorously recall the day that our whole family was busy taking off the first hay crop on our south quarter. Sister Sylvia was in the house looking after lunch preparations and I was raking hay with a small tractor, while Mother drove the larger tractor and baler. Behind her, Father was being towed along behind the baler, standing on the stooker (a metal frame to stack the bales on). As I made my turn at the east end of the field, Mom was just coming up to the crest of a steep hill a few hundred feet from me. I could see the tractor and baler enveloped in a veritable cloud of hay dust as it came over the hill.

After making my turn, I glanced back at my equipment and then over to the other tractor just in time to see the whole operation, tractor, baler and stooker, plummet to the bottom of the hill in one gigantic cloud of dust! I jumped on the clutch, stopped my machine and sat there dumbfounded, wondering what had happened! As the dust cleared, I could see Father, prying himself out from under a large pyramid of ten hay bales up on the top of the hill where the stooker had left him. Mother was sitting at the bottom of the hill with all the equipment, her head resting on the steering wheel, laughing uncontrollably!

I walked over to where the baler was. It had pushed up the entire windrow of hay in front of it, which threatened to envelope the whole machine! Dad came walking down the hill, covered in dirt and hay, exclaiming unmentionable syllables. Once she regained her composure, Mother was able to explain that as she breached the crest of the hill, she had reached to shift the tractor into a lower gear. But in so doing, her foot had slipped off the clutch at the most critical moment, leaving the whole train of equipment

123

to freewheel to the bottom of the hill at high speed!
Poor old Dad was about to trip a full stook of heavy
hay bales when the operation got away and left him
"buried in his work," so to speak!

As the years flew by, there were many other
exhilarating, learning experiences, as I recall. One
such time, while my little sister Sylvia and I were
riding on top of a fully loaded hay wagon, it became
detached from the tractor when the hitch pin popped
out of place. A freewheeling wagon with no brakes and
no steering is a certain menace, and leaves its
passengers with knots in their guts as they cling on
for dear life! The wagon hitch skipped along the gravel
road for a ways before digging in and bringing the
wagon to an abrupt halt! My sister and I were nearly
launched over the front end of the load, but thankfully
managed to hang on. We were fortunate as a family to
have never suffered a more devastating accident. Many
of our friends and neighbours lost everything from
fingers to loved ones in the dangerous practice of
farming in those early years.

I believe that the most dangerous piece of equipment
we owned was the big circular wood saw that was
used for cutting firewood. It had a blade about three
feet across that was driven by a flat belt from the
tractor. We would hoist full sized logs up onto the saw
deck and push them by hand through the saw. At any
given moment, our fingers were only a few inches from
that screaming blade, which always gave me chills. I
know of at least two men that lost fingers in such an
operation, and I paid particular attention to hand
placement for that reason.

My folks were careful to give us adequate instruction before sending us out with any piece of machinery; this was critical training needed to keep us safe. One day, one of the boys from school became stuck in a hay baler, which nearly ended his life. There have been countless pieces of clothing and several toolboxes gobbled up by rotating machinery at harvest time. These are *affordable* reminders that it could have been one of us! A neighbour from south of town flipped his tractor over on top of himself while working on steep terrain, an experience that left his children fatherless. Hence, we grew up with the practice of always looking out for danger, a practice that would surely save us from many accidents in the years to come.

My first yacht

Many interests, developed at an early age, resurfaced in later years in a more serious way. I couldn't know at the time, but even the countless hours spent building rafts and bridges on spring sloughs and the boat that I built for the farm dugout would stir in me a keen, nautical interest that would eventually take me across the world. Polling along on some flooded lowland in the spring on my makeshift raft was my prelude to sailing on the high seas. There were countless, imaginary encounters with pirates as I explored imaginary South Pacific Islands. Rarely did I come home with dry rubber boots, having tested the waters and finding them deeper than they looked. Mother only shook her head in silence. (I suppose you could say that the depth of my wisdom at the time could be measured by the height of my gumboots.)

125

When I was eleven years old, my father explained to me how the action of a boat's propeller resembled the operation of our grain auger. It didn't take me long after that to scrounge up a section of old grain auger shaft. With this piece of scrap, he taught me how to make a screw, or propeller, for the barrel boat that I had built for the dugout. Dad proudly coached me with the construction of this simple little motorboat and bravely gave up the use of his Clinton grain auger motor to power my little craft. Many a happy day I spent churning around and around that pond in my boat, learning some of the basic dynamics of watercraft. Mother always wondered at my fascination with the water and worried about me the days I was down along the flooding creek or exploring alone along the fast-flowing Peace River. These were great days of learning and vision building, and ultimately led me to join the Navy at the age of seventeen. Sailing across the world on a 366 ft. destroyer was vastly different than my homemade boat, but was somehow a natural progression of my interest.

During those farm years, we were fortunate to enjoy the friendship of Joyce and Lloyd Cook. Unknowingly, they contributed to my mechanical education by virtue of the fact that they stored their snowmobile out on our farm. That old Sno-Jet greatly enhanced my winter exploration and enjoyment. This winter fun prepared me for years of snowmobiling and winter operations, as I would eventually come to serve with Provincial Parks. The early snow machines had very small engines compared to the machines of today. Some snow machines used only one-cylinder, eight horsepower motors to get along, but still we had fun. Learning the detailed mechanical functions of a machine can pay dividends when trouble arises. Many years later, my life would be saved by that very knowledge.

The joy of family adventure

I had been setting cross-country ski trails in the park on Lesser Slave Lake, when my machine broke through the crust of a wind swept drift. Out along the lakeshore in -30° howling winds, I struggled to keep myself from freezing. I was operating a 900-pound twin track snowmachine, towing trail grooming equipment behind. Being too far from my truck to attempt to walk back, and with my radio battery frozen and darkness closing in, the only option was to dig my way out. The wind increased as I shovelled a long ramp in the snow to get back up on the surface again. As I worked, gusts of cold wind covered my tracks and grooming equipment with snow. I had to pack the ramp and let it harden several times before successfully climbing back up onto the surface of that huge drift again. It was careful use of power and balance and an understanding of snow dynamics that eventually got me free and back to the warmth of my vehicle.

One day, my boy Trevor lost his balance on our snowmobile and ran into a gigantic spruce tree. The impact shook the tree so hard that it promptly unloaded a veritable avalanche, leaving Trevor and his machine buried in a mound of snow. I believe I laughed for an hour! With his incredible balance, Trevor enjoyed skiing behind the machines when the snow became deep enough. Just as I had done, my kids would spend countless hours driving and skiing, enjoying the great fun our northern winters have to offer.

Chad, my youngest boy, often came with me out into the park to help set miles of cross-country ski trails. He would pull a packer ahead of me while I set cross-country ski track behind. Together, we enjoyed a most spectacular wonderland of snow and forest along the scenic wilderness setting of Lesser Slave Lake Provincial Park.

My fondest memory of snow machines was of a night run, far out onto the lake. Riding beside me on another machine was my daughter Julie who had become quite a proficient rider while operating a snowmobile for the Arctic Winter Games held at Slave Lake. At the limit of our run, we shut off our engines and enjoyed the sheer silence and pristine beauty under a star-studded sky, far from the lights and noise of society. I think we lingered out there until after midnight, talking and enjoying the beauty of the land.

Great family enjoyment results when everyone can suit up and get out on snowmobiles, dirt bikes, all terrain vehicles or some other form of outdoor fun. Our family enjoyed many trips into the Slave Lake wilderness on snowmobiles and quads. During a wet year, the backcountry trails are simply linear mud bogs with miles of challenges and fun. From our acreage on a Sunday afternoon, we would take several quads and explore the fifteen or so miles to the historic Grizzly fire tower. Arriving home in the evening gave our family a day packed with adventure (and mud).

For several years, I drove a full sized van as a family vehicle. We camped, picnicked, canoed and even went motorcycle camping. With a van or a camper, one can pack in as many youngsters as you have room for and head for the quiet of the forest. This is my idea of ultimate fun. On one trip to Morton Lake on Vancouver Island, I had eight little people crammed into my camper (that was all the seat belts I had). When in northern Alberta, my boys and I used to load three dirt bikes into the van, along with gas and tools, to go motorcycle camping as far from the city lights as we could get. As a family, I believe we are all thankful for the freedom we have to enjoy this great land we know as Canada.

My wife Maggie and me enjoying Lesser Slave Lake in –30 degree temperatures.

Chapter Six

Seasons in the sun

A most delightful characteristic of the northland is that each season comes expressively equipped with the power of sound, smell and feeling. These are the attributes of the land that become ingrained in your senses and bid you to share in its pulsing existence. Despite having lived much of my life since then in urban areas, the *joy of the land* continues to draw me outdoors. I guess this is where the saying, "You can take the boy out of the country but you cannot take the country out of the boy" originates from. Having been raised in close proximity to the wild and being able to experience the heartbeat of the land, one becomes a "Child of the Land." It is a distinction that becomes an integral part of you, influencing for a lifetime, your thoughts, worldview and a desire for peaceful living.

Homestead social stimulation

Our good neighbours, the Newlands, socially enhanced those first years on the farm. Frank and Mary and the kids lived only a gunshot away on the half-section, east of ours. They had two busy young lads in their family, and I became friends with the elder, Arnold. There were only a couple of years that Arnold and I were able to play and explore together, but that short time helped form our social skills in this remote place. As little tykes, we could barely find our way to one another's house, while our mothers could see one another from their respective front doors.

Arnold and I were always safe, exploring the garden and raiding the peas and the sweet baby carrots under the hot Alberta sun and the watchful eyes of our mothers.

Arnold and me, carefree in paradise!

I can still visualize Mr. Newland, one winter, out on a frozen slough in the field across from our house with his little Caterpillar tractor. He had a stone boat, a kind of land raft, chained to his machine, playing crack-the-whip out on the ice. While the boys howled with pleasure back on the stone boat, Frank sat firmly planted on the Cat with one steering brake locked back, causing the whole thing to spin radically on the frosty surface. I later heard that he caught *you-know-what* from his wife Mary for doing that!

We learned to never let hard times and difficulties prevent us from seizing every opportunity to enjoy life. Little pioneers might find their fathers out on a frozen pond after a hard day's work, labouring to clear snow from a patch of ice so that the youngsters could learn to skate. Typical of many Canadian families, many hundreds of hours would be spent playing endless games of shinny hockey or fox-and-rabbit out on the pond. Evenings were seldom without the joyful company of our families or visitors engaged in non-stop card games. Hundreds of steaming pots of coffee were consumed over deep, profound conversations and political debates. Seldom a week went by without live entertainment provided by someone's musical parents playing the *squeezebox* accordion, guitar or perhaps a violin or banjo.

We spent many evenings listening to the old tube radio on the kitchen counter. Father would carefully tune out the squeals and static radio clutter to bring in the news or a radio play for us to listen to. Mr. E.C. Manning was Premier of Alberta in those days, and we would often hear of his famous leadership exploits in the province. If we were to tune in again on Sunday morning, we could again hear Mr. Manning as he preached a sermon over the airwaves as a church minister. There were also daily updates on what was happening across the Pacific in Korea as our country played an active role in the war.

I retain a vivid memory of going to town, one wet spring day with the Newland family. Unlike today, when we dash to the car and motor in comfort and speed, we had to prepare in advance for that five-mile trip. The ladies got all dressed up, which of course meant no long underwear or gum rubber boots. Hats and purses were dusted off and arranged, while the kids had to endure the lecture on how to behave while in town.

The men had to warm up the Cat, or the tractor, and chain onto the stone boat to make the trip. In the winter and spring, they would have to bring water and a charged battery to start the pickup truck that was parked a mile away along the correction line road. With the men driving the noisy Cat out ahead, we children clung to our mothers and tried desperately to balance in the centre of that lurching drag, floating behind!

Since there were still no roads that far out, we had to follow our meandering Cat trail through the woods and sloughs. When the Cat's tracks sank out of sight in slough mud and water, little boys would scream with delight. And our mothers ... well, they just screamed! The Cat, being heavier, sank deep in the muck while the wooden stone boat floated safely on the water and sludge. By the time we arrived at the correction line road only a mile and a quarter from home, our family was already muddy and tired.

Out along the road, Father kept a 45-gallon drum of fuel and a gas pump near our truck that we had parked there, and it is refreshing to reflect that to our knowledge, no one ever attempted to steal fuel from us. The men would go to work getting the old truck fuelled, started, and turned around on the slippery, clay roadway. Then we were off to town in speed and style. If you have never experienced riding in an open pick-up truck box on a muddy road in the spring ... well...um, unless you particularly enjoy doing laundry, I wouldn't recommend it! Our mothers were not very impressed, but as kids we were having great fun with the fall-out of little mud balls thrown from the truck wheels.

Once in town, we were all made to behave, whatever that meant, while we went shopping at the store. If we were good, whatever that meant, we might get a peppermint candy or even a piece of tasty cheese from under the big cheese glass in Mr. Audet's general store. Soon, however, it was back home again with long faces and bagfuls of necessities like garden seed, salt, sugar, yeast and coffee. I can vividly remember the novelties such as a bag of Puffies Cereal at least as tall as I was, and a five-pound bag of macaroni, which at that time cost an exorbitant 29 cents!

Before the government had constructed secondary roads in the district, every mile of travel was an adventure. When the trail out from the farmyard was dry, travelling was no less than a bumpy trek through the bush, over stumps and roots, around water holes and fallen trees. Changing northern seasons, however, ensured that this was not the usual experience. Fortunately, the vehicles of that era with their high clearance and tall, narrow wheels were well suited for the task.

Most often during spring or after a summer rain, the trail was a slippery, muddy challenge of fighting the wheel to keep the vehicle from dropping into deep ruts and water holes. If the wheels slid back into the muddy ruts made from the last trip, the vehicle could be hopelessly high-centred and your journey was abruptly over.

It was during those wet seasons that our tractor or Mr. Newland's Cat was most often used to get through. Whether it was by vehicle or with farm machinery, getting stuck was a *skill* that we all learned at an early age. Once the machine was thoroughly buried and all hope of extraction was exhausted, one simply hiked back home or to the nearest neighbour for help. Thus, despite the annoyance, getting stuck occasionally resulted in a cup of hot coffee and a welcome visit.

Appreciating distinct seasons

Even when travelling along graded roadways, the Peace River gumbo mud could become so sticky and balled up that the vehicle's wheels finally couldn't rotate any longer. Attempting to continue could only be made at the risk of burning out the clutch, so the only option left was to roll up your sleeves and dig out the fender wells by hand. Consequently, we didn't always make it to town in pristine fashion! The mud was never permanent, however, because Alberta is famous for its days of bright and beautiful sunshine. Soon, the puddles would be steaming, the birds singing and plant life growing in prolific abundance.

Seasonal changes in the north are distinctive and very predictable. Winters are cold and long, but generally characterized by days of blazing sunshine. Only the onset of a blizzard seemed to dull the bright of winter. Later in my childhood, I learned as an outdoorsman to fashion cardboard glasses with thin slits to see through. These were designed to prevent snow blindness when outside for a long time in the bright sun and snow.

Snow rarely lasted past Easter, so from March until April there was a period of cold bleakness that was the least favourable season of the year. With the snow slowly melting, but not warm enough for plants to grow, this pre-spring was a depressing cold and colourless season that we simply endured. This was the time to savour the good memories of winter and to anticipate the coming of a glorious spring.

Without exception, a northern spring was always worth waiting for. The migrating birds flocked back in waves of species, while hibernating wildlife once again crawled back out of their dens into the bright sunshine. The skies became busy with countless 'V' formations of wild geese, cranes and trumpeter swans flying north for the breeding season. After a long winter, it was always exhilarating to hear the calling of the returning wild geese and other migrating birds. This annual migration brought closure to winter and the promise of warm days ahead.

The wait for spring seemed endless, until one day you might sense that the dormant tree trunks were finally getting just a little greener. Suddenly, wonderful new life and *spring green* seemed to explode all around you. The runoff water seemed to flow everywhere, and tufts of green grass and spring flowers bravely peeked out from the cold ground. Life emerged from winter in fruitful anticipation this way each year, and was never disappointing. Despite the hardships created by flooded fields, great puddles and long muddy roads, spring was a refreshing season that we all enjoyed.

Each year, as the land began to dry, thoughts turned to what we could plant for crops. Dad would always perform a germination test on the seed grain he

138

planned to use. Laying out a strip of cloth, he would count a specific number of seeds of each kind he intended to plant. Covering that layer of seeds with another piece of cloth, Dad would keep them moist, warm and dark until the seeds began to poke through the top layer of cloth. When the time was right, he would solicit my help to count the number of seeds that actually germinated and began to grow. Deducting the amount that failed to grow would establish an indication of the percentage of crop success we could expect. We did this with wheat, oats and barley. This exercise gave me my first lessons in planning.

Dad also wisely planted about 40 acres of small seed such as Red Clover or Alsike, which would require only minimal management and harvesting. Some years, the clover seed was an extremely good price, and in other years we stored the seed and waited for the price to rise. The Red Clover frequently proved to be the cream of the crop, so to speak, because when cereal grain prices were lower, the small seed prices were often high. These legume crops were also an excellent replenishing agent for the land, maintaining the wealth of the soil. Learning these facts as a child were, for me, good lessons in management.

Summers in the north were short, but hot and memorable. A familiar saying was, that while standing in the middle of a quiet field, one could almost 'hear' the crops growing. The further north one is in the world, the more hours of sun there are during each summer day. By mid-June, just north of the fifty-fifth parallel, the sun peeked out at about 4:30 in the morning, and we enjoyed its light and warmth until after 11:00 o'clock every evening. With these long, hot days, we were able to grow crops that would have required a much longer growing season a thousand miles further south.

By the end of June, our first hay crop was already rich and tall. This was an especially valuable crop, because the first cutting of hay was the richest and would become the late winter feed for the cattle. By August, the outside temperature could be in the 80°F (26°C) range, which would quickly ripen the crops. From that time on, farmers would begin to watch vigilantly for an opportune time to begin harvest.

Before it was time to harvest, however, each farmer would mechanically overhaul and lubricate the equipment in preparation for a busy harvesting season. From that time on, we anxiously kept one eye on the weather and one on the crops. Not paying attention meant that you might miss a small and valuable window of opportunity that may not be regained. Once the decision was made to begin the harvest, we were intensely focused on the job in order to remove the crops before the onset of winter. That was often an extremely anxious and tiring time of the year, as we all tolerated long, dusty days and very little sleep.

In Alberta, the fall season could be a colourful and exciting time if the weather cooperated. On the other hand, it could be a depressing disaster if the fall rains refused to give you a break. In bright, dry years, the crops were harvested in record time, the garden produce was brought in and canned, and our family was well supplied for the winter.

The greatest part of our earnings, which came from cereal crops, was very critical to the survival of the family. "Making hay while the sun shines," is a phrase that means more to a farm kid than anyone. It speaks of the need for good discipline, prompt, wise decisions and decisive action at the correct time to obtain success. It is no wonder, then, that farm kids rarely fail in other areas of life, having once learned such valuable lessons.

Once the crops were harvested and as much produce as possible was sold or stored safely out of the weather, we turned our attention to the preparation of the land for the following spring. Each field was worked up so that it would dry quickly next spring. Some of the straw was gathered for bedding for the cattle, and the harvesting equipment had to be winterized before the snow fell.

It was in the cool months of October and November that I remember a wonderful sense of accomplishment and peace. With the whole year's work on its way to market, we could settle back and enjoy the sheer beauty of the fall and make further preparations for winter.

Deciduous aspens painted the landscape with extraordinary colour while the aromatic spruce and balsam remained a fragrant green. All the forest animals were busy storing their winter's food supply, including the black bears that foraged on whatever they could find to fatten up for hibernation. This was the prime time for game bird or big game hunting, which would help supplement the food supply and provide healthy, wild meat for the winter.

As the last of the autumn leaves fell and the fields were cultivated, our cattle were brought in from the pasture. A full tank of fuel was ordered in and firewood was cut, split and piled, ready for the long, cold months ahead. By the time the last of the snow geese had flown south, the ponds were frozen over and delicate, fluffy flakes of snow began to fall.

The land became even quieter at this time, as though breathless with anticipation, and the whole land was primed for winter. As the earth became clad in white, some of the brightly coloured birds that we thought should have caught a flight south, remained for a while, singing and playing in the sparkling snow. The outdoors seemed alive with crystal perfection, and the crisp, clean beauty would uplift one's heart. Winter had once again arrived in the northland!

By late October, it was cold enough that snow usually stayed and often would not melt away until the end of March. This meant that we could count on five long months of winter. To look on the bright side, that meant five months without mud or mosquitoes or most other annoying insects, for that matter.

Cold weather is cleansing by design, especially during periods of extreme, cold temperatures in the forty to fifty-degree-below range. Nature seems to use this cold to eradicate certain unwanted parasites and germs.

The winter season was not a time of idleness, however, because for farmers, this was the time that they fattened their steers and other animals ready for market in the spring. Hay crops had been carefully stacked in such a way that moisture from rain or snow would not spoil the feed. The hay was then measured

142

out to the livestock as needed. So long as the animals were protected from the wind and supplied with water and food every day, they continued to grow healthy and strong.

Dairy operations were also ongoing throughout the winter. Milking the cows and feeding pigs and chickens was a part of every day's chores, something that farm kids learn early. This is great training that builds self-discipline, which in return, is a valuable virtue for success in any future endeavour.

Some farmers, like my uncle Bob Hampton, also maintained a trap line to supplement their income in winter, and some of these men harvested as many as 1,500 furs per winter. My father didn't trap but taught me how, so that in my pre-teen years I would have a source of winter income to depend on. Though I disliked taking the life of these little furry creatures, I knew that it was an acceptable way for people to make a living. Trapping, in those days, was simply a type of profitable harvest, not unlike our hog or cattle operations.

Winter was also a good time to rebuild equipment if a shop was available. Being ready for the next planting season was always of paramount importance, so equipment was kept in good repair to prevent breakdown at a critical time. This was an industrious but peaceful atmosphere in which to grow and learn as a child, and nature had a large role to play in our understanding of life.

The family business

Being immersed in and very much a part of the family business, is also an exceptional and valuable learning experience that has life long benefits. This kind of life teaches one about teamwork and sharing of responsibility. It teaches one to be patient and continue with the work for months or even years until the final goal is reached. You also learn quickly what your own particular gifts and talents are, as the work is so vastly diversified.

I have heard people say that as we are born, that is what we will be. I believe, rather, that to a large degree, we *become* who we are as a result of our surroundings and the input we receive as children. It is paramount to teach a child how to make good choices at an early age. These learned skills will help him develop, to discover his limitations, and build a life of success. Now, from the perspective of an adult, and looking back on those impressionable days, I can see how each circumstance and lesson served to shape my character and the way I now think.

Chapter Seven

A man ain't a man without wheels

Once I walked, but now I ride,
I traveled slow, my time to bide;
I yearned to know how freedom feels,
And love my life since I got wheels!

D. Greenfield

When I was very small, my parents gave me a tricycle to ride that was just fast enough for my infant courage. I soon wanted a bicycle, and so, talked my poor old overworked Dad into modifying my tricycle. He dutifully went to work and mounted one of the little rear wheels in the middle of the axle at the back, and presto! I was the proud owner of a two-wheeler. The pedals were still on the front wheel, however, and when sharp turns were made, the rear part of the tricycle frame would hit the ground. This created some attention-grabbing moments and kept my Mother's first-aid practice current.

It wasn't until a real bicycle became available a few years later, that this odd looking bike was put away. When I did finally get a proper bike, the country somehow shrunk as my love for exploration grew.

Country dirt roads could be quite pleasant to ride on when dry, but became more challenging when wet or while riding in the dark. Unlike pavement, dirt roads hold the imprint of every vehicle that comes along; the heavier the vehicle, the deeper the imprint. When riding a bicycle, one had to carefully balance between the ridges of the tracks on the road without getting your wheels caught. Wet days were completely out of the question, as were icy winter days, although I did once invent a set of chains for my bike tires so that I could ride on the ice. This worked marginally well until I got trapped in a frozen tractor track and performed a grand face-plant in the middle of the road. After that lesson, I devoted the winter to skiing.

A boy soon learns that freedom comes with wheels, and as an old gentleman once said, "A man ain't a man unless he's got wheels." My bicycle gave me that freedom for quite some time, but eventually I began to feel the need for speed. The creek hills helped accomplish this for a time, which again depleted the first-aid box. Then came experiments of tying my bike behind my dog Laddy with a long rope. After that, I attempted roping up to the tractor and even the truck, one day. (That one hurt!)

My homemade motorcycle

Finally, in a fit of desperation born out of the need for greater speed and mobility, I challenged Father with this dilemma. "I need a motorcycle." A motorcycle would, of course, cost money, which was a scarce commodity, so buying one was out of the question. The only option left was to build one, so I detailed a plan that my dad patiently listened to. I could visualize the little engineering wheels turning in his brain, and his eyes glazed over as he settled back into the chair. Moments later, rising silently and taking a couple of enormous strides toward the back door, he motioned for me to follow. Excited now, I scampered along behind, full of anticipation of what he had in mind. (It's all in whom you know, they say, and I believe that to be true!)

Dad and I shuffled through the collection of old bike parts behind the garage and dragged out some select sections to the shop floor. He thoughtfully worked and planned as I jabbered on in the excitement. Finally, he shook his head, saying, "Nope...no good...not strong enough. We need a big bike frame for strength here."

With that, we dove into the old truck and roared off to our neighbour's place to inspect their supply of retired bike parts. Finally, we found that Mr. Pelletier had a couple of old bike frames rusting away behind his house. Rene, however, was a giant of a man who had to duck his head just to get through the kitchen door, so his old bike frame would be far too large for me, I figured. Dad thought for a while, and then with a smile, pulled Rene's rusty frame out of the weeds, chucked it into the truck box, and we headed for home. I sat in silence, partly in bewilderment and partly in fear of what Dad might come up with!

Within a couple of days, he had motor brackets welded onto the frame with a large wooden pulley cut out of plywood to fit on the back wheel. He cleverly used the small 24-inch wheels from my old bike and fastened them to the large 30-inch frame we had procured. Father employed the use of our Clinton grain auger motor again, ingeniously fastening it to the brackets on the bike frame. We found an old "V" belt from the combine to extend from the motor to the large pulley on the back wheel, and just like that, I was the proud owner of a motorbike. Wow, was I proud!

To say the least, the bike was a little rough in the early stages of its development. To begin with, we used a wooden thread spool from Mom's sewing drawer for an idler pulley. That got me around for a short time, but was responsible for a three-mile walk home one day when the spool disintegrated. Little by little, Dad and I refined the machine until it was fast and reliable. Eventually, I removed the bicycle pedals and mounted wooden running boards so it looked like a real scooter. This made me very popular at school, since everyone wanted a ride on my new bike. Proudly, I became the first in my school to have my own wheels, and my new motorbike gave me a greater degree of freedom.

Motorized now, I learned to compromise, trading the joy of the wilderness peace for the exhilaration of speed and noise, not to mention the bug collection in my teeth. If there was a problem, it was the tires. The Alberta government, in an attempt to create all-weather roads had spread sharp, crushed gravel over the clay road grade. This truly did make durable all-season roads, but sadly, at the expense of windshields and tires. My bike tires were only designed to carry the weight of your common freckle-faced kid, and not for this heavier motorized conversion. This again presented me with some regular exercise as I blew out many a tire. In frustration, one day, we cut the bead off an old tire and installed the whole thing inside a new tire with the tube on the inside of that.

Father on my homemade motorbike

This was the day my tire problems ended, and serious, extensive exploration resumed.

That little two-and-a-half horsepower motor could scoot me along at a blazing 30 miles per hour, a definite improvement over my pedal bicycle. Although it didn't have gears, one could still slip the belt on the hills or increase speed or power by adjusting the fuel jet on the engine.

Again, I learned to compromise, as the gentle, fragrant breezes of bicycle riding were replaced with howling wind and the sting of collisions with bumblebees and other insects at high speed.

My friend Dick was envious of my newly found fun, and in no time at all, sweet-talked his father into a motorbike as well. He came riding across country, one day, proudly sporting a fancy new Moped, ordered in from the Eaton's catalogue. In the days that followed, the two of us rode many miles together and had mountains of fun exploring with our machines.

I cannot remember how many years that little home made motorcycle served us. Dad would use it to ride out and check his crops, and I rode that tired hunk of iron every chance there was until it was finally worn right out. By that point in time, I had studied every motorcycle on the market and had determined exactly what I needed next.

Compromise

There were very few motorbikes around that I liked except for a throbbing *250 Norton* or a rare, sleek

Indian, but what I really needed was practicality. Not great speed, but cross country ability; yes a dirt bike would be the answer!

The next spring, with practiced perfection, I whined to my folks about my needs and they in turn, gently redirected my thinking to see the difference between actual needs and frivolous wants. To my deep regret, my desires turned out to be the latter, which meant I would have to wait until I had earned enough money to buy the thing. (The way I worked, I knew that could be a long while!)

My regret was promptly followed by exasperation, so there was nothing left to do but sulk. There's nothing like a good sulk to pacify one's aching heart, unless you include kicking things or throwing tantrums which seem to only prolong the agony.

Barely a month went by before my hope was again bolstered. One day at suppertime, Mom and Dad launched a tentative offer with a plan for me to earn the necessary money to purchase my dream bike by fall of that year. (I'm sure they held their breath while I contemplated their offer.) For them, it could mean getting some actual physical work out of their explorer son, or, it could result in a long lower lip and more sulking. That was a chance they would have to take.

I took the bait. Yes, there was no doubt that given the lack of resources, this would be the only way that I could achieve any serious freedom; by working! It was a horribly foreign concept, but thankfully, ushered in a very valuable turn of events. As a teenager, I had learned a list of unmentionable words that were not acceptable in everyday conversation, to which I had consciously added the word *work*, and strived to avoid it at any cost!

Thus far in life, I had lived like a king, helping out where I must, but having virtually everything supplied for me by my very capable parents. I always did what was asked of me in the way of chores around home, only to fulfill my great desire to suit up and explore the land. This exploration was an ambitious pursuit that had encompassed every season, expanding my love and awareness of the great outdoors and consuming every possible waking hour of my life.

All that summer, I worked for Dad to earn the money to buy my new motorcycle. I helped extensively with seeding in the spring, cutting and baling hay as well as harvest and fall cultivation. That year, as part of my new job, I had to figure out how to budget for fuel, budget my time and plan ahead from week to week for the farming business. All the while, my new dirt bike hung like a carrot in my consciousness. Those long hours on the noisy tractor, ploughing or cultivating, cutting and raking hay, I spent pre-planning expeditions for that new bike.

My parents were friends of the Co-op store managers in town, and when harvest was over, Dad ordered my new Suzuki trail bike at the amazing cost of wholesale plus ten percent. Judging from the time it took for that prized cargo to arrive, it must have been back ordered all the way from Japan! When it did arrive, it seemed like eons before the rain would stop and we could get to town to pick up my dream machine. My heart still pounds whenever I recall that moment. There was my new Suzuki, all chrome and knobby tires and calling me to leap aboard! Dad painfully forked over the inconceivable fee of three hundred dollars that I had earned, and we rolled it out the door.

After two frustrating days of pre-ride maintenance on my bike, I developed unkind thoughts for the person who had written the instruction manual. I am sure the writer had never been a kid, nor were they well versed in the English language. Finally, with Dad's help, I learned how to install the lubricating oil, grease the wheels and chain, as well as tighten all the loose parts in preparation for the first ride.

Oh, to know freedom! This was my dream come true, and from that time on, there wasn't a trail or road anywhere in the country that didn't have my Suzuki tracks on it. The bike had a handy carrier on the back, to which I fastened emergency supplies and spare parts. I even invented a handy rifle rack to carry not one, but both of my guns for hunting season. I took my responsibility seriously when it came to supplying a share of the food for the family, and game birds were plentiful throughout the long, crisp autumns.

On rare occasions, I travelled far out to the northwest. Following trails and forestry cut lines I could meander my way to a most spectacular canyon. This was the confluence of the Burnt River and the mighty Peace River, which created a vast canyon. A haven for songbirds and wildlife, this amazing place was virtually alive with nature and a joy for me to visit. My faithful trail bike would get me far enough down over the breaks (crevasses) of the riverbanks to be able to watch wildlife movement in every direction. It was always prudent to keep an eye out for sow black bears with cubs, but other than that, there was very little danger.

The memories of all that I have seen and enjoyed by that peaceful canyon will be cherished forever, and I am so very glad that I didn't have to stay at home watching television.

That little motorcycle served me faithfully for many years and became such a part of my existence, that there was barely a single day when it was not ridden. Alvin, our little dog, would often ride along, sitting on the seat ahead of me with his feet on the fuel tank. To put all this travel into perspective, it should be explained that I seldom rode that machine without the large trail sprocket installed. This sprocket gears down the bike so that it is slower and more powerful for trail riding. By the time I sold my faithful Suzuki, I had logged over ten thousand miles at a speed of less than 30 mph! On the infrequent occasion that the highway sprocket was installed, I could travel an amazing 42 mph (going downhill with a tail wind!)

The Grey Ghost

Learning how to generate some cash flow gave me a new freedom that I hadn't known before. I now wanted a car to drive, so went to work and busily earned and saved my money for several months. When my tobacco can piggy bank was just about full, I struck a deal with my friend, David Donaldson, to purchase his 1937 Chevy sedan. What a car! My mom loved it and wanted me to restore it. However, there were other plans floating around in my inventive mind.

After driving the car home, I began to work on my secret plans for this thirty-five dollar investment and as the weeks went by, my plans became evident, much to my dear mother's horror. First, the dash and interior were disassembled and then the body was unbolted from the frame. After that, I removed all the parts that I wanted to reinstall after the body was off and ready for the final modifications. With the help of the tractor, Dad helped me lift the body off the frame, leaving me with only the bare frame to work with. Slowly, my new dirt buggy took shape with some innovative welding and fabricating. I had to borrow one headlight from each farm tractor so that the car had lights again. The original dash was reinstalled out in the open and I manufactured a little deck on the back, mounting the fuel tank on top of it, which gave me greater clearance over rough ground.

A month later, when my beautiful dirt machine was finished, my mom cried. "It is so ugly!" she protested, "and has no protection from the rain or snow. Why, it doesn't even have fenders!" she complained. That last problem was one that I had not factored into my construction plans, and would result in a face full of mud on more than one occasion.

Despite the unrefined appearance of my new car, it was a lot of fun to drive, even if it was somewhat impractical. Even Mother enjoyed driving it, taking lunches out to father in the field. Scamper and Alvin, our trusty dogs at the time, would happily sit up on the fuel tank on the back, enjoying the wind in their faces. We did have to be extra careful, though, when travelling through cow pastures. There were ominous patties of cow manure here and there that quickly became airborne when run over, a distinct hazard when one has no fenders!

This car became my long-range vehicle, "going where no boy has gone before," so to speak. My Chevy had no body, and therefore no paint or shiny parts. People in the country called my dirt buggy "The Grey Ghost," because you could see only the dust it made.

This became the greatest hunting and exploring machine I've ever owned, not only because of its natural camouflage, but because it would actually haul quite a load. On rare occasions, I would go hunting with my friends, who would stand up in the open breeze with their shotguns at the ready.

I could never afford good grip tires, of course, and without the weight of the car body, that buggy had no traction. I always carried a shovel, a rope and a good jack in case I got stuck in the mud. On the other hand, being so light, it would also move like the wind, which was kind of dangerous without the protection of a windshield. I once collided with a bumblebee at 70 miles an hour, which nearly knocked me right out of the car!

'41 Coupe

My next big expenditure was yet another car. Of course, this took another year or so, because with all the fun I was having there was barely time to earn any more money. This new (old) car, a sleek, 1941 Plymouth five-passenger coupe, cost me a whole forty dollars. To my mother's delight, I did fix it up and paint it (albeit by brush). This was a smooth riding, powerful classic with a Chrysler six-cylinder flathead engine that would give me lots of fun and experience.

Father allowed me to construct a racetrack around the edge of the wheat field where I could hone my skills at speed and cornering. My '41 Coupe was big, heavy and stable, and gave me good training that would last a lifetime. Naturally, during the process of learning, there were a few mistakes made. Dad would ask what had happened out on such-and-such a corner, and I had to confess that sometimes momentum had triumphed over skill, so that I had missed that corner! Needless to say, Father's wheat crop suffered a little, but he didn't complain. I think he knew that every trip made around the track was worth a great deal in experience.

By the age of sixteen, I still loved riding my motorcycle but was ready to explore further afield, which would require a regular driver's license. Studying the driver's handbook was exciting, because passing the exam would give me even more freedom than I had ever known. My parents helped me to study by asking me questions out of the handbook and by giving me proper driving instruction on country roads. When the day came for my driver's test, Father drove me to the town of Rycroft where the Motor Vehicle office was located. He needed to haul a load of clover seed as well, so we took the big grain truck instead of our car. It didn't make any difference to me, because as a farm boy, I was able to operate the big truck as well as any vehicle.

I nervously sat through my written exam and then went out to the truck with the examiner for my road test. He looked at me and said, "Is *this* what you are driving?" "Umm...well...yes," I stammered, as I climbed aboard. As he climbed up into the dusty cab, he gave me an odd look of disbelief. We drove around town, backed the truck into tight driveways and parked on imaginary hills.

When we were done, the examiner said, "I notice that you drove over the crosswalk at every intersection. Can you explain this?" "Crosswalks!" I said, looking around, "What crosswalks? There aren't even any sidewalks!" He then explained, "At every intersection, you must understand that there will be a white line painted on the pavement that marks the crosswalk." "Well, great," I thought, as I looked at the dusty dirt roads in town. "What do I do now?" I told him that if I had seen any indication of painted lines in the dirt, I would surely have stopped. He hesitated for a moment, and then to my relief, overlooked the infraction. When I received my new driver's certificate in the mail, it came as a "B" Alberta driver's license, which indicated that I could drive any vehicle up to and including a commercial tandem axle truck! This was an unexpected advantage of taking my driver's exam with my father's grain truck.

Suspect!

When I was seventeen, I looked after the farm while my folks went on a holiday. My responsibilities included the running of the entire farm while they were gone; feeding livestock and poultry, gardening, maintenance and daily field work with tractor and implements. I earned a whole twenty dollars for my efforts, so when my parents arrived back home again I was allowed to go on my own holiday. I had planned to visit my girlfriend and some relatives over a thousand miles away in Saskatchewan, which would be a very long trip for my little motorcycle.

After some consideration, I think my parents believed that it would be a good challenge for me to complete a trip of that magnitude, which might help to overcome some of my shyness and build some confidence. Since I had proven myself capable of being responsible for the family farm and having completed the fieldwork assigned to me, I was allowed to go.

Early into my trip on a lonely stretch of highway near the little town of Oyen, Alberta, the head gasket on my motorcycle blew out. Here I was, three days from home and stuck with an inadequate set of tools and not the materials to affect that type of repair. After whining to myself, which is always a lost cause, I pleaded with the owner of the hardware store to open up that evening and sell me a little piece of gasket material. I then pushed my bike a half mile back out to the highway service station and begged the attendant to let me use the tools in the garage. After removing the head bolts and the engine cylinder head, I traced the old head gasket onto my new material and cut the thing out with my jack knife. The tricky part was in re-torquing the head bolts back to manufacturer's specifications, by *feel*. Around midnight, the repair was complete and I camped in a nearby pasture field, continuing on the next day.

The following day, August 17th, was an arduous trip across the expansive province of Saskatchewan. By nightfall, I had come through Lanigan and was groping my way down Highway 20 in the dark. The bugs were so thick I could barely see where I was going, which made travel painfully slow. When I arrived in the town of Govan, I stopped at someone's house to ask directions to my Uncle Pete's home in the country. Strangely, no one would answer the door. Then I tried several more homes in the area, also to no avail. "What an unfriendly place this is," I thought. "Even though the lights are on, no one will answer their door." It was getting late when finally I knocked at the door of the grain elevator agent. Thankfully, he did answer and was happy to give me directions out to the farm.

As I rolled up the driveway to my uncle's home, I could see that the lights were all still on and that there were people inside. It was nearly midnight when I parked my little motorcycle and knocked at the door, only to find that no one would open the door. "What in the world!" I continued to knock until suddenly, the door swung open wide and the guard dog was let loose, growling and snapping. I was standing to the side of the door when the dog hurtled by and attacked my bike. Quickly removing my helmet, I hollered, "Hey! It's me, Warren, Frank and Margie's boy!" At that, they hauled me inside before the dog was able to get me. They all stood there, my uncle, aunt and all my cousins, white-faced and staring in disbelief. I thought to myself, "Boy, they sure must not get much company out here."

As the story unfolded, I began to see what had happened. My misfortune was an untimely arrival. Not having the benefit of hearing the news while I was travelling had rendered me ignorant of the worst random mass murder in Canada's history. Sadly, it had occurred not far away at Shell Lake, Saskatchewan, and the murderer was presently at large. It was no wonder people seemed so unfriendly that night. Here I was, a stranger, wandering from home to home, knocking on doors. I am thankful not to have been met with buckshot or have been accosted by the police, and surely thankful not to encounter the real killer. Despite the surprise arrival, my cousins and I had a good time over the next few days before travelling on to Strasbourg to visit my girlfriend.

Bees in my helmet

On the last leg of that return trip, I was faced with an obstacle that was the result of a dry year, coming in the form of thousands of flying insects, the worst of which were the wasps. I had experienced heavier concentrations of flying insects in Saskatchewan that left my motorcycle helmet virtually dripping with bug guts, but without the wasps. An occasional collision with honeybees and the odd wasp on this trip had left me a little sore from stings on my neck. But, once I arrived back in the Peace River farm country, the wasp concentration increased. Many times, between

161

Valleyview and Eaglesham, I rode right off the road and into the ditch while trying to pry my helmet off to release the angry bees inside. My helmet didn't have a face shield, so honeybees, when they hit, simply made you flinch. Wasps or hornets, on the other hand, their little bodies being much harder, felt to me that they had been shot out of a gun and nearly knocked me off the bike. Of all the tormentors, I liked the honeybees the best, because they never thought to sting before they plummeted into your face and they simply dripped off. Wasps, however, seemed to realize that if they were bound to die, their last act in life should be one of revenge, and sting they did!

Each time I was *nailed* with one of those creatures, they left me with a nasty lump, which, after a while, made me nauseous and dizzy. I kept moving, simply because there was no way to solicit help, and it was just too far to push my bike home. By the time I finished motoring up the last dusty mile of road to the farm, I could barely stand up and was having trouble breathing. As a result, I was sick for weeks in bed with a painful case of tonsillitis. Mom took me to the doctor in Spirit River, who gave me some antibiotics to curb the growing infection.

Two weeks later, he prescribed another dose of antibiotics, which still didn't help. Finally, Mrs. Osberg, our neighbour, in conversation with my mother, suggested that a topical disinfectant like Dettol might help if I were to gargle with the horrid stuff. For weeks, I had felt as though my mouth and throat were full of broken glass. Even chicken broth hurt as it went down, but within three days of the Dettol treatment, I was back to my old self again.

Thank you, Mrs. Osberg! That single experience taught me a great deal about personal endurance.

My trip to Saskatchewan had taken me over a thousand miles in two weeks of travelling and it is interesting to note that I still had a little money left of the hard earned twenty dollars that I began with!

Tricycles to airplanes

Over the years, my repertoire of vehicles grew from that first crude tricycle to motorcycles, sports cars, trucks, all-terrain vehicles and flying machines. At age fourteen, my Alberta motorcycle license was only the beginning of a list of certificates that allowed me to operate anything from aircraft to powerboats to highway semi-trailers. This progression of fun and experience spanned a lifetime, stimulated from the simple interests of boyhood on the homestead.

More than once while flying, motorcycling or just exploring, I encountered dangerous predicaments that required intelligence and ingenuity to overcome. Sadly, these were two virtues that seemed to be lacking in my nature. But, a farm kid learns that when you don't have the right equipment to address the problem, you make do with what you have. It seems that the very circumstantial action of life teaches us the ingenuity needed for survival.

Time and again, with tractor, truck, snowmobile or motorcycle, I have been in places that I should no doubt have avoided, and found myself buried to the frame. Being terrified of criticism often left me no choice but to find my own way out of the problem.

Wrapping a long rope around the tractor tire to winch my way out, or cutting tree saplings to create a corduroy bridge, meant there was always a way to make an escape.

Many years have gone by since the pleasure of my first set of wheels. I must say that the freedom and convenience have undoubtedly been worth all the expense and frustration they caused.

Recently, I was riding with my daughter Kerri in the busy city of Vancouver. She was zipping in and out of the traffic with ease as I found myself nervously hanging on. Sensing my uneasiness, she smiled and said, "Relax, Dad, it's *me* driving." "That's not the problem," I said. "It's that you...well...drive like I do!"

Chapter Eight

Things you don't tell your mother

Exploring far from Mother's side,
She'll never know how hard I cried
When caught within the river's swell,
I almost died, but shall not tell.
D. Greenfield

There are things that happen in a boy's life that are best not mentioned if you don't want to worry your parents. In my case, it was my Mother whom I was particularly concerned about, and I was quite aware even from childhood that she watched me carefully and worried a great deal. My mom was a keenly intelligent woman with a great sense of humour, capable of fits of laughter that would render her completely unable to stand or continue the task at hand. Mother had great patience when listening to her children and stayed focused to answer our unquenchable inventory of questions.

She did not, however, mince words; what was right was right and you had better learn it the first time! (This is what keeps your mental pencil sharp.) Quite often, Mother illustrated her teaching with meaningful but descriptive words and word pictures. Some of these words, however, were not classified as acceptable communication in public. At any rate, we learned which words to add to our everyday vocabulary and which ones to use when no one else was around. Overall, my sister and I were never in doubt as to the sincerity of Mother's love, even if she did on occasion use stronger than normal language to express her intent.

As a small boy, my first indications of her concern were expressed when she found me in places where I should not have been. Here, I was scolded, or in rare and deserving instances, given a sound whack to my quivering backside, like the day that I tried to cross the log bridge when I was two years old and found out what it meant to be grounded. Or, the day she found me riding precariously on the front of the hayrack while the threshing crew was hauling in sheaves. She scolded me as well as poor old Dad for that one. She did not like her four-year-old so close to the pounding threshing machine, nor did she like me being around the fidgety horses for fear I might get stepped on.

Father wisely did not tell her about another incident in the field that same day. I had been roaming around, trying to stomp on the mice that were escaping from the oat sheaves as they were being loaded. While the horses were standing still, I ran underneath the team and became trapped when one of the horses stepped back onto my foot and just held me there. Fortunately, Dad came along looking for his little bandit boy before moving the team and the hay wagon. Had he not done so, the heavy wagon would have rolled right over me. I was scolded and warned that I had been lucky, because had it been a cow that stepped on me, I would surely have been badly hurt. It was then that Dad sat me on the front of the rack with my feet through the boards so I couldn't get into any more trouble.

Weapons training

Have you ever noticed that mothers always worry when fathers put weapons into the hands of youngsters? Once, Dad brought home a little bow and a set of suction cup arrows that got me into royal trouble. We had company that day, and the house was busy with boring adults, so I went hunting with my little bow. Of course, the best targets were live ones that I shouldn't aim at, so I was left to hunt imaginary ones. Finally, I spied the kitchen window through which I could see my mom standing at the counter. If I could just sneak up close and aim right at her head, my little arrow would stick on the window, and that way my live target wouldn't get hurt. From the bushes, I pulled back on the bowstring, took careful aim and let the arrow fly. To my dismay, it disappeared entirely! (I think I exclaimed "OH SHOOT," or some reasonable facsimile.) Instantly, there came a yell from inside the house along with some nasty words that I have since learned were not acceptable in mixed company. With her hand held up to her head, Mom came to the window and yelled, "Warren! Was that you? Get in here right now!" Oops, that did it!

After my bum cooled off, I was then firmly restricted to shooting at non-breathing targets, which I discovered was much safer than shooting my mom. I argued that she kept the window too clean for me to see if it was open or closed. This didn't seem to help with my defence, as she was standing there with an obvious red ring on her forehead where the arrow had stuck.

When I was about ten and old enough to go hunting, Dad took the time to teach me all there was to know about owning a single-shot rifle. We took it apart and put it together again and learned to aim and how to hold it steady, and the most important part, where the safety catch was. After some shooting practice he told me some stories about how he learned to hunt and how he could shoot two prairie chickens with one shot, and challenging stuff like that. Then, since it was late in the day and the bush partridges would be feeding along the edge of the field, he sent me off around the quarter section with the .22 rifle in hand to fetch supper.

Well, did I ever feel like a big guy! Out hunting with all my new knowledge and no less than two .22 calibre short cartridges in my pocket. About a half hour into my hunt, I saw a ruffled grouse up in one of the trees at the edge of the field. I quickly loaded a shell into the chamber and pulled back hard on the hammer to cock the gun. While I was fumbling around and grunting, trying to pull the hammer back, the silly bird chickened out and flew off. I did finally manage to get the hammer back by sticking out my tongue and using both hands. I was thankful that I hadn't shot myself in the foot, and the bird was thankful to be smarter than I was. Rather than repeat that episode again, I simply left the gun cocked and continued sneaking around the edge of the grain field.

When I got back to the farmyard, I walked boldly over to where Dad was working at the lumber pile, and handed him the gun in no particular safe fashion. He gingerly grasped it in two fingers, held it up, looked at it, then said, "Do you have a bullet in there?" "Yup," I said, stammering to get the story out. His face went kind of pale as he pointed to the safety catch. "It's off," he said, kind of quietly. Oops, I forgot about that part. He released the hammer and slowly pulled the bolt back and the shell dropped out onto the ground. As I picked it out of the dirt, he said in a louder voice, "You could have shot me!" With a scolding, the bullets were taken from me and because of that grave mistake I didn't get to hunt again all fall. Again, thankfully, Mom was never told.

On one occasion, when Mother asked me to get a chicken ready for supper, I thought that if I shot it with Dad's rifle it would be far less painful for the chicken than my chopping its head off with an axe. So, I sneaked out with the gun, took careful aim...and fired. Oops, shot the wrong darn chicken! (Sorry about that.) It only got worse, however, as the first shot took a leg off, the second shot wounded it somewhere else and I finally had to chop the head off anyway because it just wouldn't die! Mom asked me what took so long, and I believe I used one of those occasional departures from the truth to explain it. (Close, very close...)

Of course, the older one becomes, the more mischief one can get into and the more stories you have to tell your friends, but wisely, never your mom.

Laddy and I were out exploring far from the farmyard one day, and were about half way across a very large beaver dam when we spotted a black bear. Strangely, my dog didn't see it right away, so I quietly called him and just crouched down there on the dam, petting my smiling dog. The bear was routing through a rotten log, looking for ants, and luckily we were downwind. I was pinned down and didn't dare get up and move, or the old bear would have seen us for sure. Had she seen us, there would most certainly have been a vicious battle. A fight like this might have killed my dog, as Laddy would naturally defend me but was no match for this 300-pound powerhouse. I am sure he must have wondered why we squatted there for so long with the air full of mosquitoes, but the bear finally had enough and moved on. By the time she did leave, it was getting very dark and I was overdue for my chores, so we scampered for home on the run.

An exciting May long weekend, when my Aunt and Uncle arrived from Edmonton, my cousin Ray and I were out target shooting with his new fibreglass recurve bow. That thing had so much more power than any of my homemade bows and could drive an arrow right out of sight, which unfortunately, happened on more than one occasion. So, finally tired of target shooting, we said to ourselves, "I wonder how high it could shoot? Hey, there's an idea. Let's try that!" So, Ray pulled back on that powerful bow as far as he could, and like Nimrod of old, shot his arrow straight up to heaven. Like a couple of dummies, we stood there for a moment, squinting into the sky, saying, "Can you see it? No, do you see it? No, I can't see it." Then, in one moment of panic, our eyes met and we yelled, dropping the bow and running madly in opposite directions. Whew, that was close! What goes up must surely come down! We escaped that falling arrow, but sadly, it being our last one, somehow didn't come back! I believe we determined, like Nimrod, that one shouldn't shoot at God or he will keep your arrows.

Dead wrong!

On a cool fall day, when I was thirteen, Dad and I went moose hunting along the breaks of the Peace River. Each year, most northern families would harvest a wild moose to feed them throughout the long winter. This was the first time I had hunted moose alongside my dad. We first determined exactly where each of us would walk and that if we shot an animal, we would signal the other with two quick shots in the air. Dad hunted to the north of me by a quarter of a mile as we stealthily walked parallel to the river. After an hour or so, I sneaked up the back of a little sparsely treed hill and peaked over the other side. My heart raced, because quietly grazing in the valley below was a cow moose, identifiable by its lack of antlers (I thought). It was a good hundred yards away, so I had to steady myself and take careful aim to ensure a killing shot. The last thing I wanted to do was wound the poor thing and send it running for the bush. I breathed slowly, focused carefully and squeezed off a deafening round. The .303 bucked hard, and to my amazement, the moose fell instantly to the ground. Not wasting a moment, I leaped over some deadfall trees and ran down the slope. The animal began screaming its head off and I was on my way to end its pain as quickly as possible. After dispatching the moose, I stood there in the snow trying to catch my breath, when suddenly I heard a tremendous crashing in the bush. I knew it was entirely too big and noisy to be my dad, so in a panic, I scanned the area for a tree big enough to climb.

To my horror, I found myself in a stand of willow and young poplar trees, none of which could carry my weight. As my heart sank, I turned back toward the source of crashing trees just in time to see a fully-grown cow moose bearing down on me like a freight train in the night! I fired a round over her head, quickly reloaded and took aim with trembling hands. The sound of my shot halted her charge and she stood there only a few yards away, glaring down on me. At that moment, there was no hope of pleading innocence, with her one-year-old calf lying dead on the ground behind me. The air was cold and I could see her breath as she panted and surveyed the situation. Fortunately, she did not attempt revenge, as full-grown moose have been known to destroy a pickup truck when they were protecting their young.

With trembling knees, I stood there trying to remember how many shots I had left and keeping my aim steady in case this monster decided to charge. She made a fearsome sight, looking from me to her calf and then back toward me with her ears pointed back and her body steaming in the cold air, but slowly, she backed up and turned away into the bush. With my heart pounding in my ears, I sat on my warm catch and calmed my nerves. Finally, after signalling Dad, I checked my magazine to see how many rounds I had left. My mouth dropped open! The magazine (bullet clip) was completely empty! I had been far from ready for an incident such as this and nearly paid for the mistake.

A while later, Dad came walking up, smiling, and exclaimed that he had found where I made my shot, found my spent cartridge, but strangely, couldn't find another of my footprints for quite a long way. I guess I had been kind of excited! I also learned that day that yearling Bull Moose may not have antlers and yet appear to be full grown. The other lesson I learned was that one should really consider how far the meat will have to be carried to get back out to a road somewhere. I recall that it took a very long time to pack out my 500 pounds of moose meat through the bush, over deadfall and creeks!

Racing into trouble

Throughout the years, there were a variety of foolish vehicle infractions that occurred, and thankfully, never got found out. One day, I was chasing a coyote with my first car, a cut down 1937 Chevy sedan. I never planned to run the creature over and had no intention of hurting it, but was interested in knowing how fast it could go. Each time my car came up on the frightened animal, it would look around for some place to escape and looked right at me. Out in the open fields, there was no place to hide or escape, such an

173

unfair chase. The coyote would dodge this way and that, so I had to be very fast on the wheel and the brake to keep him ahead of me. Some people did chase animals and run them over, which I thought was a very stupid and insensitive thing to do to a live creature. My folks had a lot to say about others who were cruel to animals, so I never told them what it felt like to get that close. As I think back now, I am ashamed of that chase. I let the coyote get away, of course, but the look of sheer terror in his eyes will remain with me all my days.

Another fall day, while returning from a hunting trip with my *dirt buggy* car, I had a full load of wild chickens on board. With my .22 calibre rifle and my 16-gauge shotgun on the front seat, I was breezing along with feathers swirling out behind in the dust, when suddenly, the district Forest Ranger flew over me with his plane. He was so close to me that I felt the wind from his propeller! This was the Conservation Officer of that day, so I knew that if he were able to land ahead and stop me, there would be big trouble. Immediately, I swung my car off the road and out across the fields. He gave chase for a while, but soon decided that he didn't have a hope of getting me stopped, and to my relief he let me go. I think that we were supposed to have a license for hunting game birds, which I was lacking, and if there was a possession limit, I surely didn't know what the law stated. I was simply a kid, hunting to keep the freezer full for my family.

Coming back from the river, one day, with my dad's new Studebaker sedan, I came across another kid from school. He was driving his dad's new wide track Pontiac and challenged me to a race. Well, in the face of peer pressure, I buckled, which was unusual for me, but began the race anyway. My folks never knew it, but I got off the line quickly enough to get ahead and stay ahead. This is an extremely critical move to accomplish when one is racing on loose gravel roads, because the car behind inevitably gets showered with rocks and will suffer severe damage. I got away that day, not because I had more power but because I got ahead and fought to stay in front and away from the rocks. I never tried that again with my parents' car. I simply couldn't risk the embarrassment of damaging that vehicle and having to face my folks as a fool.

A couple of years later, my buddy George and I were out again, looking for fun. He was driving his "new-old" 1957 Dodge and enjoying the stability of that great boat of a car. Along came some young fellow from the neighbouring town of Wanham and challenged us to a race. Now, George was a guy who could never back down from any challenge, so away we went, speeding through the backcountry on dirt and gravel roads. We chased one another for about ten miles. At times, the old Dodge was ahead with rocks flying out behind, but then the other guy got ahead and left us in a veritable meteor shower of gravel! There were pieces of glass flying in off the windshield and hitting us in the face, but ole' George would never back down. His motto was that you never, ever give up, no matter what! (I often worried about that guy.) Finally, on a long, outside curve with pedal to the metal, we came up neck-and-neck with the other car. We both noticed the speedometer at that point, and the old Dodge was cruising at 120 miles per hour (200 km)! Then, with a smile and a wave, the race was over and we parted ways.

When we got home, we were both still wired on our own adrenalin and jabbering like chipmunks. Our friend, Norman Barnhardt was sitting there in the kitchen having coffee with my dad as we spit out our story, still talking faster than auctioneers. After the story was done, the men just sat there quietly looking at one another with their feet apart, coffee cups in hand. After a minute or so, Norm said in a dry, quiet voice, "Wasn't it the '57s that used to have all the front-end trouble, Frank? You know, when the front wheels fell off?" That did it. George and I both jumped up and dashed out to inspect the front end of the old car!

I'm sure the men got a chuckle out of our white faces, but we never heard another thing about it, and I sure didn't risk any more foolish high-speed chases (not in the old '57 anyway).

Our tour of horror

Halloween night usually rendered a barrel of fun, and each year we became a little braver and dared to take greater risks, all in the name of fun. One memorable October, three of us lads decided that the countryside had been quiet for long enough. Dick came along with his dad's old blue pickup truck with a grain chopper in the back, so we used that to escort us on our tour of horror. First, we sneaked up on Peter Poohkay who lived in a cabin across the creek from our place. Peeking through his cabin window, we could see Peter lounging on his bunk, reading the newspaper. As a precaution, we stacked up a pile of old oilcans outside his door, so that if he did come out we would be forewarned of his coming. With security in place, we were then free to prowl around looking for mischief. Peter was well prepared, as there was really nothing that we could find to play a trick on him anywhere in the yard. Someone suggested that we let the air out of his truck tires, so we crept over and were busily trying to pry the caps off the tire valves, when there was a mighty crash at the cabin door! As our security alarm went off, Mel hollered, "Run!" and we dashed for the darkness of the open field. A moment later, a whizzing sound went by over our heads, followed by the booming report of Peter's .308 rifle!

No doubt he first thought we might have been a rummaging black bear. We ran as fast as our legs would carry us, out across the ploughing toward the road where we had hidden the truck. Seconds into the escape, we encountered a most unexpected obstacle.

Suddenly and strangely, the ground completely disappeared from under us! Frightfully, we were airborne for one breathless moment before crashing into the ground again at the bottom, tumbling end over end on the frozen mud and ice! I'm sure Mr. Poohkay was well entertained by the noises of fear and exasperation that came out of that recent excavation as we clawed our way to the top and continued our escape. You see, he had ordered a new dugout to be excavated that fall so that the winter snows and run-off would supply him with a fresh water supply by the next spring. It was that great black hole that we ran blindly into like absolute fools, and I will never forget the terror of it.

We drove around for a while, trying to muster the courage to try another trick on someone. When we finally got up nerve, we left the truck out on the road and hiked the quarter mile into the Burroughs farm. Being very quiet and on the lookout for something to trick them with, we crept very close to the house. Dick spied the master electrical switch on a power pole in the middle of the farmyard, so we devised a plan to knock on several windows at once like gremlins, then pull the power off and dash for safety.

A great plan usually requires a great deal of deliberation and consideration, neither of which we took time for. This was a mistake that would soon bite us back, literally. Dick went around the north side of the house, Mel went around the back and I took the south side. At the pre-arranged signal, we all began rapping on the windows like goblins in the night. Then Dick quickly broke away, dashing for the power pole while Mel and I picked our way through the darkness back out to the driveway again, quite amused with our prank. When the power switch was pulled and the yard light went off, we laughed. But not for long, because seconds later, Morris let the family dog out with a distinct order - - "Sick 'em!" to which the obedient mutt chased us with growling and gnashing of teeth all the way back to the truck! Dick and Mel dove into the cab as I leaped into the truck box, with the dog snarling on my heels! When the old Ford sputtered to life, we left in a cloud of flying gravel and dust, off to find a safe place to catch our breath and rest our burning lungs!

When we finally stopped and were debriefing the last blunder, Dick exclaimed, "OH NO, we are really in trouble now!" Someone had stolen the grain chopper out of the back of our truck while we were playing tricks at the Burroughs place. "Oh no...oh no," he kept repeating. "My dad's going to kill me for sure!" We went back and looked all around where the truck had been parked, but to no avail. With trembling knees and fearful hearts, we drove back along that dirt road, wondering how we would ever explain this to Mr. Schmidt. Then, we noticed a dark object in the field near the road. Stopping to investigate, we discovered to our great relief that it was our lost chopper. Oh man, were we ever relieved, thankful and light-hearted once again! That just didn't seem fair; while we were busy tricking, someone else had played a trick on us.

How could we ever trust to leave our truck alone again, especially on *this* night the way things were developing? This had become our own night of horrors with pain that we could still feel! That was quite enough reverse trickery for one night, and at this point, smart men would retire to the safety of home, correct? But then, no one ever said we were smart. No, can you believe we hadn't yet had enough pain and fear? We were to hit not once, but twice more that night.

The next big strike, at the Wenger farm, resulted in Mel and Dick running at full tilt into a page wire fence in the darkness. I escaped that one to some degree, but had to nurse my buddies back to the truck again with the wind knocked out of them. How can I ever forget the sound of squealing wire and popping staples on that crisp, dark Halloween night, as my two friends bounced off that page wire fence at full speed? That historic scene occasionally crosses my mind and still brings a random smile to my face.

Our final hit was somewhat successful as far as trickery goes. We tied the victim's car to a power pole just in case he decided to give chase. Then we went to

179

work being a general nuisance. Part way through the operation, we got caught again. RATS! We lit out across the open field toward the road and back to our truck. Just as I had left the farmyard at top speed, I caught my foot on some dark object protruding from the grass, performing a magnificent face plant in the dirt. That fall left me gasping for breath and spitting out dirt and blood. "That's it," I said. "We're done for tonight." "Agreed," came the willing reply of my buddies as we sped off.

A couple of minutes later, Dick yelled, "It's not finished yet! We are being chased!" We craned our necks to see who it was, and sure enough, they had untied their car and were out to teach us a lesson. "Go faster!" we yelled. "This is an old truck!" Dick yelled back, as he wound her up into high gear. "Where in the world can we go to lose this guy?" Mel exclaimed. I thought a bit and then said, "I know the perfect place." "Where, Where?" they yelled. "Watch closely!" I screamed. "Just up ahead!" "They are gaining!" hollered Dick. "Turn here, turn right here!" I yelled, waving my arm to the right.

We careened off the road into a rough field and continued at high speed. To our dismay, the pursuing car bounced through the ditch and continued following. "They are still after us!" Dick yelled. "There is a narrow bush trail right up there, if we can find it!" I said. "They would never dare follow us in there, it will tear all their chrome off!" Finding the trail in the darkness, we sped wildly through this narrow winding track, with branches crashing off the engine hood and doorposts. With visions of large, angry Frenchmen giving us a royal thrashing if we ever got caught, we frantically raced on through the bush trails. Making a wild turn, we came out on the field again and then back into the bush on another trail, gaining speed. Panting, Dick said, "I think we've lost them. I don't see their lights." As we neared the top of a small hill, I yelled, "Kill the lights! Stop the truck!" With only the sound of our hearts pounding, we sat listening for evidence of pursuit, but all was quiet. Then Mel said, "I think I hear them, over on the main road." Sure enough, they were driving slowly along, waiting for us to emerge again from the bush trail.

For quite some time, the men drove back and forth, waiting for us to show ourselves, but by now we were all out of adventure and energy. Perhaps we were even getting smarter, so we relaxed under the bright stars, telling old Halloween tales as we waited for our pursuers to cool off and leave. Eventually, we eased the old truck out of the bush and back home again, crawling quietly into our bunks in the wee small hours of the morning.

Snow tunnel disaster

On a winter weekend, when staying over with my buddy George, we received an enormous dump of snow. By the time Monday came along, we were wading in snow nearly three feet deep and the road grader had yet to plough the school bus route open. Not having to go to school, we enjoyed the time off and went out to enjoy the winter wonderland. We got shovels out of the barn and dug our way down the driveway so that the bus could turn around when it did come. We discovered that the main road ditches were already full of snow from previous snowplough runs, which, with the latest blanket, made an incredible depth to work with. Having time and material at hand, we began to plan an extensive snow tunnel system. For two whole days, while we were out of school, we worked on our tunnel, building rooms and even towers with turrets on top. We dug at least 20 yards of stand-up tunnels, so that not only the farm dog, but the big old ram would follow us down under the snow. On the third day, it had started to snow lightly again and the temperature warmed up a little.

There was still no hope of getting to school, so we continued to expand our frozen empire along the road ditch. Just before lunch on Wednesday, we were hunkered down, resting on our snow bunks in the main cabin when we heard a strange, droning sound. Puzzled, George and I looked at each other, wondering what could make that sound. We lay there for several minutes, speculating what it could possibly be. When we finally got up and lazily poked our heads out of the turret, George shouted, "Oh no! We are going to die!" I took a frantic look down the road, and there, roaring toward us was the district snowplough with the wing (side blade) down over the ditch.

Lloyd had that big grader at full throttle, with snow being thrown all the way into the bush at the side of the road, and here we were in that very ditch under the snow! I can tell you that we never moved so fast in our whole lives. Running, we just barely made it out along with the dog, when the maintainer roared by over top of our frozen empire! We lay gasping on the driveway, watching the big grader as he manoeuvred around, and Lloyd, with a friendly wave went back up the road again. For a moment, our hearts pounded from that close brush with death and then mourned the thought of having to go to school the next day.

Suddenly, we sat bolt upright, and in unison cried out, "Where is the sheep? Oh no, he is still under the snow!" Our shovels were also under the snow, so we dug and dug by hand to open up the one end of our tunnel. We could only get a little way along before we discovered that large areas of our under-snow empire were now collapsed, which drove us into a sheer panic. Finally, we climbed up on top of the snow and poked along, looking for our top turret and a way to get down. In a moment, we found it and sure enough, it was ripped wide open and our main snow room caved in. From there, we were able to hear the bleating of the sheep, and after finding one of the shovels we were able to dig him out before the poor thing suffocated. George's dad also came out to see what had happened and helped us lift the frightened animal out from under the snow.

George and I had a number of such close calls and fun times over the years until I joined the Navy. After that, it was only a year or so before he also joined me out on the west coast in uniform. As friends, we carried on right where we left off earlier, living life to the fullest.

A quest for excitement

During my teen years, some of us boys in the area became avid skiers. Not that we had any clue how to ski. No, we simply pointed our boards downhill and hung on! Melvin was my most faithful skiing buddy. Mel had *real* skis but I started out as most farm boys did by building my own wooden skis out of 1 X 6 lumber. I used old belting to make straps to support my boots, and a welding rod down the middle on the bottom to keep the ski going straight. I steamed the ends of the boards in a bucket of hot water for days before bending them with clamps in the cellar steps. By winter, they were all painted up and ready for action.

Most of us learned to ski by dragging behind the tractor or car on the snowy roadways. Our parents would go along and visit in the warmth of the car while we enjoyed the flying snow behind. By tying the toboggan behind with a rope, we could also take our little brother or sister along. Those of us with skis would zoom back and forth on our own long rope, having a complete blast in the winter sun. This was great fun so long as you kept your skis out of the culverts or didn't get too far over the bank and break through the crust into the soft snow in the field. We became so good at this that Dad could make a turn with the car, and us boys could ski around the corner without stopping.

Once, when Melvin and I were skiing and sister Sylvia and Mel's brother Allan were on the toboggan, Dad made a 90 degree turn with all of us behind. He could see Mel and me pulling hard to one side to make it around the corner, so he turned back to the wheel and accelerated down the road again. We were fine, of course, but Dad had forgotten the toboggan with the younger kids on board. It naturally cut straight across the ditch through the soft snow and got caught in the drainage culvert. The toboggan jammed hard, nose down, leaving the kids wide-eyed and yelling for help. Dad, looking ahead, was oblivious to the pending danger behind. Mel and I could hear the nylon rope stretching further and further, sounding like an over taut violin string. Suddenly, there was an awful bang with the whole front of the toboggan breaking off, sending the rope and wooden parts right over the car! That startled my dad and he jumped on the brakes! We could see little frozen tears on the kids' rosy faces sticking out of the snow, but they were alive and unharmed.

We would often signal our dads to speed up, and then we would crouch down deep into the snowy ditch with our skis and jump the frozen approaches. This was exhilarating and often gave us a few yards of *air* as we flew off the snowy jump and back into the ditch again. That last trick sometimes left us gasping for air and buried head down in the snow bank!

The long, northern winters gave us ample opportunity to get out and enjoy life in the snow, so a Friday night after school was prime time to go skiing. If we had clear skies with a bright moon, we would be able to enjoy a moonlit landscape for many hours before dragging our weary legs home again.

I would call my buddy Dick from across the creeks and set up a rendezvous time. My friend Mel would arrive and he and I would bundle up for the cold and go together with a snack and our skis. Arriving at the rendezvous, we would then wait for Dick to arrive on the other side of the river. Because of the openness of that great land, we could see him turn the corner two miles away and drive as far as he could toward us. When he could come no closer, he would flash his lights, we would flash ours, and the ski was on! Donning our skis, we would then ski the half-mile across country to the edge of the riverbank where our favourite hill was. With the winter air so cold, we could easily converse with each other for well over a quarter of a mile, so after catching our breath, we would talk

185

for a while and then race down to see who would get to the bottom first. From about 8:00 in the evening, we often skied until the moon went down at 3:00 am before returning home, happy and exhausted. There were, of course, no ski lifts except for the occasional snowmobiler who came by, so we climbed the hill each time and skied back down again, laughing and hooting in the cold night air.

The part we never told our mothers about was the occasional times that we sneaked some of their homemade wine stock out to the hill to sip quietly under the winter moon. Dick and I would each raid our mom's wine supply from the cool of the cellar. We would siphon a little off of each bottle so they couldn't tell that we had been there, and smuggled it out in an old mickey bottle. This made a very strange mixture of old and new wines of various kinds and flavours. When consumed at 25 degrees-below-zero out on the riverbanks, it could very well be a Dom Perignon. Of course, we never drank enough to make us feel too light headed, because any energy it gave us was soon burned off climbing the hill again.

That particular winter sport went on for a number of years while we were young and energetic, and sparked in me an interest in actual downhill skiing later on in life.

Chased by a trailer

There were times when stupidity triumphed over logic and I thought for sure someone *up there* was watching out for me. Such was the case on my motorcycle trip to Saskatchewan. Zooming along, trying to make the best time possible against the wind in the mountains, I nearly got run over by an enormous trailer! I had been sneaking in behind large highway trucks as they went by, hoping to gain a little more speed in the slipstream of the larger vehicle. Each time I tried this, the truck would slowly pull away and leave me once again fighting the wind with my little motorbike. On one long hill, not far out of Jasper, Alberta, I was overtaken by a large, red Coke truck that I just knew would have a great slipstream to help draw me along.

The moment this truck passed me, I quickly moved in as close as I could behind him. To my horror, as I looked down to my left, I found that there was a heavy steel trailer hitch on that truck. My next surprise was to find that attached to that hitch was no less than, yes you have it, a Coke trailer! (A very large Coke trailer!) The truck was gaining on me, and of course, so was the trailer, so I didn't waste any time planning an escape from those big heavy dual wheels that were threatening my backside! I seem to remember sitting on the roadside for a long time after that, waiting for my hands to quit trembling, humming *Jesus Loves Me* and making daisy chains with dandelion stems!

Flying gyrocopter
What goes up must surely come down!

Teenage years often distance children from their parents because of changing interests, as was my own experience. In an effort to find some common ground with me, Dad decided to embark on a building project to bring us back together again. Knowing that flying was among my many interests, he decided to capitalize on that interest, and we began plans to build an aircraft. When we finally found the affordable answer to this sport, Father purchased a partially finished airframe from a man in Peace River. (Likely his mother made him sell it!) Together, we embarked on a program to learn the skill of Ultralight flying. Father had an advantage, in that he had previous fixed wing experience, but this new plane would be a gyrocopter, an entirely different kind of aircraft. With my poor mother worrying about our sanity, we ordered books and magazines to further expand our knowledge of gyroplanes.

The practical thing that we liked about a gyroplane, besides its relatively safe flying characteristics, was that without the use of an engine it could be flown behind a tow vehicle. This would be a definite asset, given the state of our budget and the fact that neither one of us knew how to fly the thing. Looking much like a small helicopter, it would lift off and glide behind our car on a 100-foot nylon rope. Flying that little copter was the easy part; it was keeping away from trees, fence posts and power lines that became the problem.

Each sunny day that we would prepare to take the machine out, mother would express her concerns and worry that we might not return. We assured her that we were taking every precaution possible, and indeed we did exactly that. If there was a problem, it was in the procurement of dependable parts, a dilemma that would cause us much grief in days to come. Most of the professionally made gyrocopter parts had to come all the way from the Benson factory in North Carolina. Because of this, we were forced to search locally for materials from which to fabricate our aircraft. Many of our fellow gyro pilots in those days were faced with the same problem, and if we were not careful in choosing aircraft grade parts, an accident could surely happen. This brought about one catastrophe after another as many of those first gyroplanes crashed, some injuring or killing their pilots.

Gyro-gliding behind the car

Flying was infinitely more interesting than anything else I had tried, and so much fun that we practiced every chance we could. Dad, who had now invested quite a lot of money in this project, was determined to make it a safe, flying machine. His knowledge of aero engine mechanics was a definite asset and one that kept us flying long after others had given up. We were still having difficulty ordering reliable parts, however, and at times had to rely on *farmer fabrication* to get us by. Farmer fabrication is usually explained as that which is constructed with tape and baling wire!

Towing our little copter behind the car soon led to the desire to be "free as a bird" and be able to fly anywhere unhindered. With that goal in mind, Father ordered an engine for our little craft and we embarked on a whole

189

new experience. With this new engine, we were free of a tow vehicle and able to zoom noisily across the sky, unimpeded. The little engine we finally purchased was unfortunately, quite cantankerous. Benson Gyrocopters had recommended this little power plant because of its impressive weight-to-power ratio. The McCullough 72 had been originally designed for use in pilotless drones constructed for army gunnery practice in the desert. Here in northern Canada, this noisy power plant was to be employed in such a radically different application that it became entirely unreliable.

On a sunny day when my mother was weeding the garden and trying not to watch our foolish flying activities, I took off against a north wind and then circled out over the house. I waved at her, but she didn't look up. As the gyro picked up speed, I turned south and followed the dirt road below, to the far end of our farm. Banking the machine, I pushed forward on the cyclic control to lower the nose and begin a slow descent to the runway.

The craft was travelling faster than I expected, and so, overshot the end of our property by a couple of hundred yards or so. My second surprise came when I attempted to throttle back for landing and the engine completely quit! I found myself descending into a rough field with a row of tall trees between the safety of the landing strip and me! In a moment of panic, I kept the nose down to gain as much airspeed as I could, and at the last instant, pulled back on the stick and climbed out over the trees and back to the runway again. When the gyro glided in to a soft landing on the grass and the rotor speed had slowed down, my dad came driving up. He had been watching in fear from his helpless location at the far end of the field, and now walked over to me, trying to look calm. With a silly grin, he asked, "Need any toilet paper?" (I believe I accepted!)

That was a good lesson, and as we practiced, we learned how to keep the machine running smoothly, (most of the time). Because of that unreliable engine, we were never able to fly comfortably over dense forest or water, but we had a great time following fields and roads.

On a particularly cool autumn day when I was sixteen, I arose early in the morning and pulled our little copter out of the seed shed where it was kept out of the weather. Having been carefully trained by my father, I began an intricate pre-flight check in preparation for takeoff. Being satisfied with the result of the pre-flight, I positioned the aircraft, primed the engine and pulled the propeller through to complete the priming process. After flipping the master electrical switch, I braced myself for the firing of the engine and pulled the prop again, this time much harder. The Mac caught and fired on the second pull and settled down to a deep rumble, while I eased myself into the cab and buckled up. Taxiing to the runway, I further checked some of the flight gear and then hand rotated the rotor as fast as I could to give it some momentum before starting off. The sun was low on the horizon and the grass was moist from the morning dew as I throttled up. With heart pounding, I accelerated slowly down the runway, giving the rotor time to reach takeoff speed. As the air speed increased, my gyroplane gently lifted off into the cool air, but I held it at an altitude of only a few feet, which was a tactic we had adopted in case of unexpected engine failure. I landed at the far end of the runway and turned around.

Now, facing a fresh breeze, I pushed the throttle ahead, quickly accelerating to flying speed, lifting off into the wind. Again, I held the machine under a hundred feet of altitude for safety's sake until reaching the end of the runway. At this point, I banked out over the farmstead and house. The air was cool and delicious up there as I looked down over the harvest fields. I flew toward the rising sun now, enjoying the beauty of the landscape, and at a thousand feet I banked to the south and glanced down at my instruments. WHAT was that! I jumped - - there, bravely clinging to my instrument panel was a fat little field mouse! He looked down at the ground a thousand feet away and then back to me as though he was thinking, "Buddy, I sure hope you know what you are doing!" Smiling at the thought of the story he would have to tell his mouse friends, I knew that I must surely bring him back home again. Banking the little gyro over the south quarter, I eased the power off and glided in to the north. As the farm buildings came into view, the wheels gently touched the wet grass and we were back on terra firma once again. My little passenger lost his grip as the machine was taxiing to a stop in the field and he tumbled off into the grass. I wonder from time to time if that little fellow had any idea what he had just accomplished. (Do they make tiny rolls of toilet paper, I wonder?)

Dad and I flew together until the time came for me to leave home. My interest in flying, however, would continue and I eventually studied my Pilot's Ground School and enrolled in Fixed Wing flight lessons. I also belonged to the Popular Rotorcraft Association and kept up with advancing gyrocopter technology for many years after that. Joining the Victoria Flying Club introduced me to many nice people and also gave me good reason to escape my drinking friends on weekends. Even when visiting foreign ports, I used my club membership to spend time with interesting people engaged in the sport of flying. Thankfully, this was much more gratifying than wasting my time and money in a beer parlour and a far better atmosphere in which to pursue another of my interests; meeting girls!

Mother's greatest fear

Father flew for a couple of years after I left home. Mom had urged him to sell the plane now that I had gone off to sea, but he believed that it still had merit for the farming business. One day, however, his whole life was altered because of that machine. Having just installed a brand new Benson rotor, he decided to equip the machine for spraying weeds in the fields.

Taking off without a problem, he circled the farm, preparing to descend into the wind over the field. Mother was outside, and as Dad flew south along the roadway, she heard a tremendous "CRACK!" from the direction of the plane before all went quiet. She ran out into the open to look for him, but Father was nowhere in sight. After taking the car and looking along the roadway, she found him upside down in a field of barley, unconscious but alive. With her worst fears raging and tears in her eyes, Mother called Mr. Grant who was also a pilot and had flown with us. He came on the run and helped to get Father to the hospital at Spirit River. Our friend, Sonny Wells, then flew him by air ambulance to Edmonton, where Dad spent the next three weeks in intensive care.

I feel extremely sad, now that I reflect on all of the warnings that Mom had given us over the years. She was never happy with the flying project, as though she had a premonition that something terrible was going to happen. I have since learned great respect for a woman's intuition, as they seem to have a gift of insight in areas where men do not. Father suffered three weeks in a coma, after which he had to learn to walk all over again. Because of that one disaster, Mother and Dad were forced to sell, that year, ending twenty-two happy years of farm life. This was a deeply sad ending to what began as a family building project, and is a memory that grieves me to this day.

Danger on the high seas

In my late teen years with the Navy, adventure seemed to find its way into life at every turn as we engaged in

the exploits of our deployment. Many of these were experienced on classified assignments that I am not at liberty to talk about, and am relieved to know that mother was not aware of. Once, on a Naval exercise in rough seas, the XO decided to test the awareness of our Aft Watchman. Since the Captain was asleep, this particular Executive Officer thought that he would toss the "man overboard" drill dummy into the sea and have the crew on watch respond to the emergency. What he did not take into account was the fact that our crews had been working very hard and were now finally getting some well-deserved time to sleep. The other problem he was about to encounter was that we were quartering a very rough sea that would make a rescue attempt very dangerous.

I was on watch in the Operations Room when the Aft Watchman caught sight of the MO dummy in the water and sounded the alarm. The Watch Officer began to swing the ship back to where we could launch the sea boat and begin the rescue exercise. The whole ship's company was soon aware of our course change when we turned broadside to the heavy seas. With the ship rolling at 30 to 45 degrees, everyone was jolted awake and scrambling to catch equipment and personal items that were being scattered around each compartment.

When we arrived back at our original drop point, the sea was so rough that we could not even find the MO dummy in those mountainous waves. Nevertheless, our XO in command ordered the sea boat over the side. Men were hanging on to every available piece of equipment to avoid being thrown overboard as the ship struggled to maintain our position. Several attempts were made at launching the boat, but the violent movement of the ship resulted in a number of scares and some minor injuries.

Finally, with the crew exhausted, our XO ordered a fresh crew into the boat to continue an attempt of the launch. I was chosen for that final crew and took my place in the storm tossed boat. We were lowered over the side and I remember the terror of being drawn under the ship as it rolled with the sea. Thankfully, the launch crew pulled us to safety. Next, we swung far out from the boat's davit (launching cradle) and then crashed into the ship's side as we rolled back again. This happened repeatedly, so that we lost some of the boat's oars, smashed the outboard motor and cracked that heavy-duty 27 ft. whaler from one end to the other.

At last, the Captain, dismayed with the actions of the XO, arrived on the bridge and took charge of the rescue. Immediately, he began moving the ship in a great arc, towing the sea boat in the lee (quiet waters) of the ship's inside wake. We were then able to launch and successfully retrieve the MO dummy, although I remember at least thirty minutes when we were unable to see the ship at all because we were buried in deep troughs of sea swell. Suddenly, out of the darkness came our ship, bearing down on us and coming between the raging sea and our tiny, leaking boat. The St. Croix appeared monstrous as it slid past us only a few yards away, but it had never looked so wonderful and inviting to me as it did that night!

Soon, gigantic blocks and ropes were lowered to us and heavy rescue lines tumbled into the boat. My back had been hurt, the Radioman had suffered a broken arm, equipment had been lost and the boat was irreparably damaged. The forward Seaman hollered, "Hooked on forward!" followed immediately by the voice of the aft Seaman, yelling, "Hooked on aft, ready in the boat, Sir!" There was an instant surge of power as our broken little piece of security was abruptly yanked out of the black sea and back aboard ship once again. The ship then resumed course and our weary crews were once again able to rest. The reward for enduring that near fatal exercise was a sip of brandy in the Captain's cabin, as we sailed away that dark and stormy night. The incident resulted in a momentary return to homeport to disembark the injured, replace the sea boat and thankfully, *the XO.*

A year later, the ship's company was recalled to the vessel from a quiet weekend in Vancouver. With the R.C.M.P. police boat ahead of us clearing the way, the St. Croix, under orders to proceed with the utmost speed, was to conduct a federal arrest. Having been berthed far up the Fraser River meant that we had to manoeuvre through fishing boats and commercial traffic for several miles to get to the ocean again. My usual station, when entering or leaving harbour was as Blind Pilotage Officer, which confined me to the Radar Room. This day, however, I could be of little help with my radar in the confines of the river channel, and so, spent my time observing our departure from the upper deck. We surged down the Fraser, dragging fishing nets and small boats, bumping along the side. Some smaller wharfs were washed away by the wake of our rapid departure. Sirens were wailing and the ship's horn was blasting all the way down the river as we pushed aside tugboats and barges to make our way out.

We then headed to sea at high speed to join the Federal Fisheries patrol boat Tanu, far up the west coast of Vancouver Island. To complicate things, a storm was raging and the sea was very rough. We were to accost a Japanese mother ship, a giant freighter that was a freezer ship containing all the catch from the smaller fishing vessels. Along with its fleet of fishing vessels, the Koyo Maru had sought refuge from the storm inside Canadian territorial waters. Their position would have been understood and this infraction overlooked had they not continued fishing inside of the international boundary.

That morning, a crew from Comox Air Force Base had flown a routine patrol up the west coast and had photographed the group actively engaged in their illegal work. With Fed Fish leading the way, the St. Croix, who was presently part of Second Escort Squadron, an operational squadron, was sent in from the south. As a further precaution, the H.M.C.S. Mackenzie was brought in from exercise area W-601 to discourage an escape to the north. The gigantic mother ship, with lights out, was resting in the lee of some nearby islands. From my Operations Room, we attempted to make radio contact but the radio was strangely silent. Finally, after several attempts at communication, even using 2182, the international distress frequency, the Captain called for an interpreter. Chief Petty Officer Kobayashi was called to the Operations Room and asked if he would attempt to make contact in the Japanese language. Moments later, a radio response from the Koyo Maru said in English, "What is object?"

Chief Kobayashi looked from one face to the other as our ship sat broadside to the bow of this foreign giant. Suddenly, the Captain said, with a note of humour in his voice, "ARREST!" Only a minute later, we had an answer to our demand. The starboard lookout suddenly began screaming in frenzy, "She's rung on steam, Sir!" "She is going to ram us!" The Watch Officer had already ordered the St. Croix to full astern when that rusty monster slid by our bow so close you could almost have touched it. Immediately, the Mackenzie was ordered in from the north and we could hear the boom of her three-inch seventy guns firing across the freighter's bow. Within minutes, the battle was over and with no way to escape, the Koyo Maru surrendered.

Tanu came alongside and picked up a twenty-five man armed boarding party from us and proceeded to make an official arrest. Our Watch Officer and lookouts were given some time to calm their nerves over a hot coffee while we waited for our boarding party to complete the capture. The fishing fleet was sent home empty handed that day as we escorted the Koyo Maru down the inside passage between Vancouver Island and mainland British Columbia. She was detained in Vancouver harbour for over a year before the courts released her once again. Canada had, up to that date, suffered many foreign fishing infractions and had lost countless millions of west coast salmon to illegal fishing. That day, we had asserted our law, enforced our boundaries and put into motion a requirement for a new international boundary, not at the "three mile limit" but at a safer two hundred mile limit.

A close call with Davy Jones!

My last posting aboard ship was to the H.M.C.S Yukon. She was a sleek vessel, a little newer than the St. Croix and was at the time attached to Fourth Escort Training Squadron. Early one fall, as we were completing a training run into Alaskan waters and were returning to our base at C.F.B Esquimalt, we very nearly paid a visit to "Davy Jones' Locker." Now, the bottom of the sea is not at all a nice place to visit, especially for a nice ship like ours.

It was a morning watch, and I was on duty in the Operations Room. A lone Sonar man was closed up in the sonar compartment and there was a minimum crew on the bridge. The ship's company was sound asleep as we travelled, recovering from weeks of heavy training, so this should have been a quiet run home in safe waters. There was little or no shipping in the area and we were a respectable twenty miles from the coastline and any menacing rocks or islands. My PPI radarscope was clear of traffic and the sleepy morning watch was nearly half finished, when suddenly, there was an ear piercing active sonar ping from the undersea phone.

Now, this undersea listening device would not normally be switched on unless one was working with a submarine. Our duty Sonar man, however, had been testing equipment that night, had used the device earlier and had left it on. The loud sonar spike was followed by five more deafening sonar pings and then a voice message that still rings in my ears..."KILO, KILO, KILO," followed by "EMERGENCY RISE!" We both sat there staring at each other like we had just seen a UFO. With the slam of a steel hatch, the Watch Officer descended from the bridge with a crash, his face pale and his hat out of kilter! He said, "Where did *that* come from?" We both pointed to the undersea phone in silence. He made a mad dash back to the bridge before we could speak, and immediately the ship was thrown full astern. The Yeoman dashed through the Ops Room on the way to the Captain's cabin and things were flying everywhere with the force of our rapid deceleration. I scrambled to the bridge, as there was still nothing on radar, and stared out into the pale, first light of dawn. The ship's screws were still pounding in reverse and there were shouts from the men down below as my eyes adjusted to the dim light outside. Several men arrived on the bridge just then, straining to see what all the commotion was about.
Suddenly, emerging just under our bow, a great, black, steel submarine became visible, her course only a few points off of our own. As we had effectively "hit

the brakes," our duty Watch Officer had avoided what would have been a serious marine disaster. This long, black monster turned out to be an American nuclear warship in transit from Anchorage to Pearl Harbour. The submarine had surfaced without a careful scan for local shipping, believing they were alone in those remote Alaskan waters. I can recall the look of horror on the men's faces and the feeling of weakness that settled over us all, as we became aware of that close encounter with "Davy Jones."

There were many more exciting and close encounters with adventure throughout my sea-going years, much of this during classified Naval sorties. Not all of my fun, though, was found at sea. The flying and skydiving that I engaged in would also have kept my dear mother awake at night had she known. Fortunately, as a boy grows older, he begins to develop a greater sense of apprehension, no doubt a result of his mother's consistent care and concern. This was her love in action that I am thankful for, because I believe that without it, I may not be alive today.

Flying high, feeling low

At the risk of appearing completely irresponsible, I will mention a time when I was about nineteen and was flying practice runs out of Victoria International. It was a summer's day and I had flown out toward Saturna Island to have a little fun. There are high radio towers on Saturna that I liked to use as pylons and enjoyed flying as fast as I could between them. This day, as I was having fun cutting in close to the tower with my right wing low and then slamming the wheel hard to the left to make the opposite turn around the next tower, I noticed some people on the rocks below, girls of course! That momentary distraction was just enough to offset my timing by a second or two, resulting in a near disaster and embarrassment. When I lifted my eyes to locate the next tower, it was already so close to my fuselage that I could have reached out and touched it! Whew...that was too close for my liking.

As part of my training, I was sometimes sent to exercise practice-forced-landings over the farms around Shawnigan Lake on Vancouver Island. This was invigorating, as one has to glide in or sideslip in to a prospective emergency landing field and then apply full power to avoid an actual touch down. Often, I sent chickens and geese flying and cows running as my little Cessna 150 screamed off the back pasture and out over the barn and corrals. I often wondered what the farmers thought of us trainees who used the Shawnigan Lake area for such practice.

Another part of our training was practicing spins and stalls over the lake. One very unforgettable day I learned how uncomfortable it could be to have another aircraft in my airspace. After I had completed a couple of spins, I noticed a bunch of puffy clouds at around three thousand feet. They were those pretty little cotton ball clouds that look so nice against a blue sky, so I decided to cut one in half with my plane. When I looked back, it had perfectly separated and the two halves were floating apart. So, with this new-found fun, I began cutting one cloud after another until the sky was chopped up with a maze of little cloud pieces looking for a friendly wind to put them back together again. I had unintentionally tuned out my radio, which was constantly crackling with the air traffic coming from Victoria International. Then, as I climbed steeply in pursuit of another little cloud, I faintly remember an all too important radio call. A strong, professional voice spoke, saying, "Victoria, this is helicopter 2345 over Shawnigan Lake at three thousand, landing."

I thought, "Isn't that interesting, I'm over Shawnigan Lake at three thousand feet as well." Then, as I plummeted through my last puffy cloud -- AHHHH...there it was! The helicopter was a large, twin rotor Canadian Forces Chinook, which looked as big as an apartment block in front of me. I cranked the little plane to the left and dove for the lake, completing my last spin for the day. The vision of that huge rotor that almost clipped my wings hung in my consciousness for days afterward. The pilot apparently never knew I had been that close, as he was no doubt concentrating on his landing protocol. When I arrived back at the Victoria Flying School, my instructor asked how my day had been. I believe I told him that it had been one of those painfully boring days, just wasting good fuel. [You know, little by little, it is possible to learn, but why, Lord, why do I have to learn everything the hard way!]

Skydiving for girls

In addition to flying, jumping out of perfectly good airplanes became a weekend sport for me that lasted for some time. My interest in flying was only superseded by my interest in girls, and one day, while having coffee with a flying buddy, some *very* pretty ladies arrived. Noticing my immediate interest, Scott introduced me to several *lovely* members of the Victoria Skydiving Club. (Can you hear the sound of my flying career flushing down the toilet?) Within weeks of that, I had completed my basic training and was ready for my first jump. I don't have adequate words to describe what it is like to depart from that small airplane and jump (voluntarily) into thin air. My flying friends shook their heads and asked, "What in this crazy world would make you leave a perfectly good airplane in flight?" Well---I thought you should see the company I am following! Every sunny Saturday, home from sea, would be spent packing chutes and spending my money for flights up into the wild blue.

One fateful day in 1971, when our jumpmaster was one of those attractive young ladies, we lifted off with a full load of eager jumpers onboard. As we neared the drop zone, she said, "It has been over an hour since the last drop and I want to check the wind drift." The pilot, who was considerably more assertive, told her not to bother, the tower had given the wind direction and velocity when we took off. Although the jumpmaster actually has command of the aircraft, she backed down and prepared to deploy her jumpers.

I was first out, standing on the right hand wheel and holding onto the wing strut, waiting for the signal. She watched the chart, and when we were just the right distance from the DZ for the wind to carry me back to it, she gave me the signal. I was glad to get out from behind that noisy propeller, and in an arch position and counting, I dove face down for the earth.
The day was warm and sunny, the countryside over Brentwood Bay was breathtaking, but there was something wrong, something very wrong. When the chute opened, I noticed that I was rapidly being blown off to the east and away from the DZ. Pulling full brake in an attempt to drop quickly and hopefully into

calmer air, I did gain a little ground, but still I was falling too far from the drop zone. I picked an alternate landing area, and then as the wind increased, I picked a second one. Floating backward, steering into the wind, I picked a third and then finally a fourth landing spot. The wind took me over the power lines and into a residential area where my fourth alternate was the roof of a small house. Just beyond the house were fields full of glass greenhouses that made me think of "ground round" and even more determined to drop into somewhere, *anywhere* safer.

Watching behind me, while still driving into the wind, I steered for the roof. Suddenly, my feet caught the top of a huge tree, which slowed me down. I held one steering toggle down and let the other one go, causing the chute to slowly spin toward my target, but the tree had momentarily interrupted my trajectory. That brief interruption caused me to miss the roof and plummet at full brake between the house and the detached garage. You might think, "Aw, soft ground to land on," but no, it was a concrete sidewalk, and to complicate the matter, a clothesline was strung from one building to another. When my feet hit the clothesline, away went my well practiced landing stance so that I hit the sidewalk at full speed, flat on my butt! If you think that one cannot *bounce* off of concrete, you would be wrong, as I did rebound, right into the back yard and upside down against a picket fence.

A passing Sannichton police officer saw my perilous descent and stopped to see if there was anything worth saving. He flipped me over and pulled my legs out straight to inspect the damage. When he did that, I was able to catch my breath again, but was suffering a great deal of back pain and shooting pains encircling my whole body. After field packing my chute and limping to the vehicle, I headed home to my ship and to bed. Next day, I was in so much pain that I booked into the Canadian Forces Base hospital at Naden for X-rays. My diagnosis was exactly what you might expect from a fall like that; compression fractures of three vertebrate and massive bruising. The next thirty days were spent flat on my back in hospital while my back healed. The following year, I resumed parachuting again and made a number of successful descents. Each abrupt landing, however, gave me more pain, which finally convinced me to try a less aggressive sport.

Parks mountaineering

Park people love adventure and live it every day of their careers...memorable times like the fun and crazy adventures of mountain climbing, getting lost in heavy cloud cover and descending into the wrong valley. Or, dangling off of mountain sides with a full pack, attempting to take photos of places where no man should ever go! I have a great photo taken on the Golden Hinde, the highest mountain on Vancouver Island. The picture was shot downward between my feet and shows a climber below me with a climber below her and one even further down. This might not seem too serious if it were not for the fact that this was not a technical climb and no ropes or climbing gear were being used. We were tenuously clinging to rocks and shrubbery on the mountainside. Below us, the valley floor was a heart stopping 3,000 feet away! Later that same day, we were working our way across a narrow ledge of rock on a sheer cliff. The cloud cover was only a hundred feet below us, so the visibility was very poor. Right in the middle of that narrow rock trail along the mountainside was a large, round stone resting on the ledge. Each of us had to put our packs on backward and keep our backs to the rock wall to avoid being nudged over the edge while we gingerly climbed over this obstruction. I was having difficulty getting over the thing, so began to figure out a way to eliminate the problem. Prying and grunting, I finally managed to off-balance the stone with my boot and sent it plummeting into the cloud below. Our shock came as we heard the rock crash into something a couple of hundred feet down, and then all went silent. I counted...1 – 2 - 3 – 4 – 5 – Crash! Wide-eyed and staring at each other, we surveyed our vicarious surroundings with the sudden realization of our apparent altitude and got ourselves off of that narrow ledge as fast as we could!

Provincial parks provided many opportunities to test my adrenalin function. Bear encounters are interesting and often frightful, and throughout the years there have been too many of them to detail. When working in remote park areas, Parks staff were usually well prepared with pepper spray or a 12-gauge pump shotgun loaded with 1 ¼ oz. slugs. On occasion, though, one inevitably must stand face to face with your furry opponent and try not to run. We were taught never to run from a bear because that would trigger a "chase" response.

Park Ranger Doug Greenfield gives instruction at the Goldstream salmon run.

This picture was published on the front page of the Victoria Times Colonist newspaper, October 26, 1985

Now, there are many temptations in life, but I doubt any as difficult to overcome as the temptation to turn tail and dash from a 300-pound black bear, popping his jaws and swatting the earth. With trembling knees and weapon at the ready, you lower your eyes and back away slowly, talking softly to the creature. (I believe they prefer to be called SIR, at this point.) We must remind ourselves that we have encountered this majestic animal in "his own living room" and we are the intruders. On the rare and memorable occasion that one forgets the rules of the forest, that formidable resident of the wild will be sure to teach you who is who in a lesson you won't soon forget.

Cliff rescue

My most exciting encounter in the wild was, however, not with menacing wildlife but with marauding teenagers. One night, as Duty Ranger at Victoria's Goldstream Park, I received a distressing call from a group of young people who had been partying in the area. There had been a lot of activity and mischief from local teens looking for fun and excitement over the summer holidays. The young people were for the most part not causing any damage, so we tolerated them sneaking about and even enjoyed challenging them from time to time.

When the distress call came, it was delivered by a group of girls who were crying. A bunch of guys and girls had been walking along a narrow trail on the northeast side of the river, when some jostling began. Pushing one another soon resulted in one young lady disappearing into the darkness along the steep river cliffs. With kids crying and everyone pointing to the spot where she was last seen, I carefully worked my way down the slope in the darkness. Finally, with my flashlight I could see that the tracks on the sandy slope vanished over the edge into absolute darkness.

Holding onto the vegetation, I worked myself closer and closer to the edge, hoping to get a glimpse of where she might have gone. Standing on the very edge of the cliff, feet dug into the earth and gripping the stalk of a broom bush with one hand, I leaned out, shining my light down to the river below. I could then

210

see the young lady sprawled on the rocks some fifty feet down, unmoving and silent. I called to her, but as I did, I felt the broom bush beginning to pull out of the soil. Turning back in desperation, I fought to gain my balance, grasping for more vegetation. With one hand gripping my big flashlight and the other thrashing madly to find a handhold, I slipped unimpeded over the edge!

I recall that suddenly, everything became absolutely still as though caught in time. I could see rocks, dirt and branches hovering in the light in front of my face as I fell for what seemed like a minute. Suddenly and painfully, I crashed down hard at the bottom where the cliff meets the river's edge. Strangely, my B.C. Parks Stetson was still on my head and my flashlight was still in my hand. The landing had stuffed my nose full of dirt and twigs and my pant legs were forced up almost to my thighs from the fall, but thankfully, no bones were broken. Beside me, only a few feet away, lay the young lady I was attempting to rescue. She was breathing and conscious, but had a broken lower tibia. At that moment, I was very humbled, thankful that I had not landed right on her, possibly causing irreparable damage.

Making her as comfortable as possible, I then reached for my radio to call for help but it was not in its case. Searching the area, I soon found the walky-talky upside down in the river. Pulling it out and drying it off, I reattached the battery and attempted to make my call. "MEEEP..." was all the response I received. I was stranded and alone on the wrong side of the river and far from help. The young people were hollering from up above and I was fearful that another one might make the same mistake in an attempt to help their friend.

With much yelling, complicated by the echo from the riverbanks, I convinced them to stay up on top and that their friend was going to be alright.

With that, I left my coat to warm the injured girl and headed off down river looking for a way back up the cliff again. It took me a half hour to clamber and swim my way back to the trail, and it took the Langford Fire and Rescue professionals over three hours to extract the young lady from her precarious dilemma.

Provincial Parks gave me twenty-five years of exploration and fun. With training in rappelling and cliff rescue, emergency extraction from burning vehicles, off-road driving and helicopter rescue, life was never dull. Most of us were trained in forest and structural fire fighting, all-terrain and snowmobile operation and extensive weapons handling. Looking back at all my certificates, I found that by far, I had received more weapons practice in Parks than we did in the military.

These were the enjoyable years to remember, flying helicopter patrols into mountainous country, doing moose counts from the air, and building backcountry facilities with all-terrain vehicles and aircraft. Snowmobile runs across mountaintops and frozen lakes, problem wildlife encounters and unsavoury experiences with criminals were all part of the job. Countless hours of friendly rapport with Park visitors and colourful local characters, alone, would make up a book full of notable memories.

During my Park's career I also studied emergency medicine and served in the Provincial Ambulance service as an EMT. Although my training was fun and challenging there were many days that we put our lives on the line in the course of duty. Even the training was dangerous. Cliff rescue, emergency extraction from vehicles and aircraft or high speed ambulance operation left no room for mistakes.

If I had life to live all over again, yes, I would certainly follow the same fields of interest. Challenging life in the pursuit of a career that you are not expressly gifted for (for the sake of riches or other nebulous fare), will undoubtedly lead to frustration and boredom.

The greatest danger

As for mother's concern and warnings, she had good reason to be concerned. It was my awareness of her concern in my younger years, however, that worked like a compass, steering me away from the presence of inescapable danger, the kind that results in an official letter or phone call from authorities that begin with, "I'm sorry to have to inform you about your late son, Douglas Warren." Thank you, Mother, for building in me (sometimes painfully) a sense of right and wrong, and ultimately, an awareness of where adventure becomes foolishness and foolishness leads to the slippery slope of disaster.

We all love a little excitement, an adrenalin rush and a good adventure, but if I could leave you with some final words of hard earned wisdom, I see our biggest enemy and greatest danger to be "untruth." It has been said that, "It's not what we don't know that gets us into trouble, it's what we do know that just isn't true that is most dangerous." Lies are what cause wars, ruin peoples' lives, break up good marriages and families and separate nice people from the happiness that they all long for. For example, believing that drugs or booze can be your friend is a lie. I have watched good friends die and have seen many families torn apart because they allowed substances like these into their home. Also, believing that you, a mere human, are somehow more important or more valuable than some of your fellow humans *is* a blatant lie! To think that there are really no standards for right and wrong is also a lie.

Politics, marketing, news media and some religions will use untruth to further their cause. These are all things that we will experience in daily life. Therefore, always tell the truth, be informed, learn the truth and be able to make intelligent, informed choices. Personally, I have suffered more pain and disappointment because of lies than any other destructive force I've ever encountered, bar none!

Finally, for you male readers, "Never, ever attempt to date more than two girls at once, and never, ever, lie in wait to crash an all-girl nurses' wilderness retreat without trained backup. No matter what your age, you <u>are</u> too young to die!

Chapter
Nine

Backward
brainwaves

There comes a day in everyone's peaceful childhood that Mother says to you, "You're a big boy now, and guess what, by this fall you are going to be able to go to school!" The first question I asked was, "Did Tarzan go to school?" to which Mother must answer, "Yes, of course, dear. How did you think he got so smart?" At that point, although you are only five years old, you have a sense that these last bright months of summer may be the only days of freedom you have left for a very long time.

My folks provided very well for me before school began, but I suddenly discovered that I was at a great disadvantage, this being that I was too small and dreadfully ill-equipped to run away from home before school began. So, here I was, stuck with the first great dilemma of my life. Shall I go to school and get smart like Tarzan, or should I stay home and pursue a career as a vagabond? Mother looked at me sternly, glanced at the punishing strap hanging on the wall and quietly informed me that it would be in my best interest to get an education. Ok then, that's it, my mind is made up. An education it is! Whew, school didn't look so terrible after all, and of course, it was still several carefree months away with much exploration to be done in the meantime.

Life sometimes has a way of short-circuiting your best plans, which inevitably happened early that summer. Just when the July sunshine was at its grandest and the forest was warm and alive, someone decided that the little Greenfield boy should have a chance to interact with other children before school began in the fall. What! I gotta go where? No, Mommy, I can't leave all my animal friends down at the creek! "An' I ain't a 'posed to go to school till fall!" I protested.

So, they dressed me up in silly clothes and I rode into town with my dad, who was at the time, temporarily employed with building an extension onto the school. Mother explained to me that I would be going to a kind of play school, a thing called DVBS. Well "D-b-v-s" or whatever it was called was cutting into my prime summer exploration of the creek and I was working on a good long lower lip.

When we arrived at school, a strange lady came to meet us who was all sugar coated and sweet-talking and dragged me off by the hand to meet the other children. Sitting on the floor, I made myself as miserable as possible, hoping above hope to be sent home quickly. My leather shoes were tight on my feet and not nearly as comfortable as my Indian moccasins. My play clothes were gone, I had to wear tight, fancy town clothes and besides that, I wanted to be mad!

So, I cried and cried until the lady went and got Father, who embarrassingly took me home again. As soon as we got into the truck, I began to feel much better, slipped off my shoes and put on my biggest smile. (You have to reward you parents now and then, you know.) Dad lost an hour's work while he drove me home and presented me to my stern faced mother. She stood there with her hands on her hips and proclaimed, "There is just no way in - - (some where very hot) that he is going to stay home!" (Possibly, just possibly, Mother was upset with my decision to leave school so soon?)

Oops, she saw right through me. I hated it when she did that, and I was in trouble, now! Down from the wall came the strap, so I scampered to the truck and put my shoes back on in a flash. Mom then came into town with my dad and I and promptly unloaded me at the school with that ominous bulge of the strap still in her coat pocket.

While Mother looked on smiling, sugar lady met me and cooed me like a baby. After this turn of events, DVBS got quite a lot better. After a time, they gave me a project to paint, which as I recall was a picture of a little church with a steeple. The other kids seemed nice enough, and after a while it became almost enjoyable, not at all comparable to the quiet of the forest, but I guess sometimes you have to leave civilization for a time to appreciate what you have to come back to.

DVBS accomplished what it was supposed to and I became more accustomed to having other kids around to interact with. Here was where my first lessons in daydreaming were cultivated, a skill that I would so desperately need to combat the boredom I was about to encounter in grade school.

September came all too quickly and school clothes once again became the dress of the day. Mother took me to school on the first day of grade one with *the persuader* in her pocket again. That whole first year for me was intensely miserable. My teachers had every hour of the day detailed out, which left no time for freedom or exploration. Sitting at a desk, making little marks on paper was only fun in art class. The rest of the time, it was beastly boring and I could barely wait to catch the bus home.

When recess came around, we had a short reprieve from studies only to meet some even worse challenges in the schoolyard. A number of our students spoke only French when playing with their friends, which caused some segregation on the playground. If you couldn't speak French, which I could not, they would not allow us to play with them, and therefore we felt like outcasts. In 1956, the French population in our school was decidedly larger and expressly more domineering than the rest of us. As the years went by, English did finally become the normal schoolyard language, thereby diminishing the segregation considerably.

Cigarettes
the passport to the outhouse

Another even larger problem was that of trying to get to the outhouse, as there was only one boys' toilet and one for the girls. Several of the big boys would hide in the toilet and smoke homemade cigarettes. This was a real problem for the little guys who needed to "go" but who were not strong enough to fight their way in. I can recall several occasions being gathered up by the supervising teachers and sent back to the classroom without a *pit stop*. No wonder my first report card mentioned that I had trouble sitting still in class!

At the beginning and end of each day was the bus ride. If I thought school was boring, this was twice as bad. It travelled for many bumpy miles to the north and west, returning back over the same route before bringing me home. This got me home almost an hour and a half after leaving school! The ride was almost unbearable for me, as I longed for the freedom and the peacefulness of my farm. The one thing that I did like

219

about the elementary school days is that the bus would drop me off a mile from home and leave me with a delightfully quiet walk in the beauty of the country. This rich time of exploration often got me back home just before supper. (Yet another bonus.)

Today, our students are outfitted with handy backpacks to carry lunches and books. In 1956, however, most of us packed our lunch in a lard pail with the lid pressed on, containing all that we needed for the day. At some point in the middle of each winter, a Native lady would come to the school and take orders for Indian moccasins. She would have us put our foot on a piece of paper, draw around it and put our name on the top. This was the order! A few weeks later, everyone's new, smoked moccasins would arrive to replace our old tattered ones, and for weeks afterward, the whole school smelled of the pungent aroma of new, smoked leather. Although they only cost a couple of dollars, this fabulous footwear was the most comfortable that I have ever known. They were warm and soft and allowed our feet to grow unrestricted.

As the years went by, school never ceased being scary for me. When there were competitive programs going on or exams that required my study, I became so nervous that I would be sick to the stomach. Many times, I got sick while waiting for the school bus, or sick at school, and my parents came to bring me home again. It was simply fear; fear of making a mistake and being scolded for it, or, horror of horrors, appearing stupid.

The reason for my fear of school was primarily a lack of self-esteem. With my self worth at an all time low, whenever I was around people, I was afraid to speak or try anything new just in case I did something wrong. Eventually, my stomach became stronger, and thankfully the fear sickness left me. During the years that followed, however, the uneasiness never really went away and I envied so many of the other kids that were self confident and bold.

So much for a doctor's prognosis

In the fourth grade, at the teacher's recommendation, my parents hauled me off to see the doctor in Spirit River to see what was causing my extreme shyness and lethargy. I was scared spitless and sat there trembling while he poked and probed, looking for a clue. In the end, Dr. Law suggested that my heart rate was a little fast for a boy my age. Well "duh," I guess so, "I'm scared half to death." So much for *his* wisdom and education! Other than that, I appeared to him to be a normal boy. This revelation did not help much either, as I was still struggling desperately to define the term "normal."

By the time junior high came into view, school was definitely getting better. By now, they were offering classes that were actually interesting, like science and social studies. Next to art class, these were my all time favourites. When the bell rang, the class would dissolve to the ball diamond or the skating rink as I slid unnoticed into the library. Here, I found the precious, quiet time that I needed to explore the world on my own again, at my own speed. It may seem strange that the school library held much of the same attraction as the wilderness, but it did. It was here that my mind could entertain any subject that was opened in front of me without interruption. Away from the noisy playground, I could be free in the quiet of my own thoughts to imagine whatever I wanted and try on each character I read about.

An accomplished pacifist

When we were required to participate, it was to play team sports, which I never did learn to much appreciate. If ever there was a place where one could make a blunder and get scolded, it was on the playing field or in the gym. Children are often cruel with their words and actions, so if a mistake was made, the retribution was often bitter. Consequently, they *chose* me as an outfielder in virtually every ball game, never Captain or Pitcher, although I could throw a mean ball. I was the player that they least wanted on their team and the feeling was mutual!

I did not have a physical handicap but there was not even an ounce of competition (not to mention interest) to be found in me. Fighting for anything was out of the question, as I was an accomplished pacifist, so hurting someone was beyond my ability, whether in word or action. As a result, my lack of interest in team sports was a continual disappointment to my teachers.

Individual sports, however, were entirely different. Give me cross-country skiing, hiking, cycling or best of all, "exploration," and I was in my element. Even track and field was better because I competed one on one rather that in a group. On any field trip, kids grouped together, chatting and exploring. I, on the other hand, would be a half-mile behind, intently studying the world we were visiting. (It was quieter back there.)

Test tubes and story telling

Such was life throughout school. I became an escape artist, avoiding the crowds and coarse talk of the other boys while hiding in the predictable, passive world of books. Unlike any of the other boys in my class, I seemed to have the strangest interests, like keeping flow charts and graphs of weather and temperatures. I did this for many years as though I were a junior analyst of some type.

Another of my interests was current events and politics. I cannot remember a time in those school years that I did not know all the names of the men in leadership in our country and in places around the world. I kept a scrapbook of pictures and articles about world leaders and events that were in the news. Even by grade two, I was aware that Mr. Louis St. Laurent had lost the position of Prime Minister to the Conservatives when Mr. John Diefenbaker took office. In grade four, I kept newspaper clippings of the building of the St. Lawrence Seaway project and its grand opening and I followed closely the first acts of violence of the FLQ in Montreal when I was yet in grade eight. Grade eight was also the year that Mr. Lester B. Pearson became our Prime Minister, bringing the Liberals back to power in Ottawa. By grade nine, I was beginning to think about world travel and followed the exploits of our troops posted in Cyprus. Next to Social Studies and art, Science had become my best subject. At home, my bedroom dresser was cluttered with a collection of glass beakers, test tubes, flasks and microscope inspection slides. My windowsill held experimental plants that I was attempting to graft, one to another. Parts of old radios and electrical components littered my closet while I experimented and dreamed of inventing some new and wonderful device to make life easier for mankind. Still, at school and at home, I was reminded of my lot in life as a "dumb kid" who could not keep up to the academic average.

If there was one thing that I was appreciated for on the playground, it was my story telling. On any warm day, I could attract several gullible youngsters to join me on the sunny side of the school while I articulated imaginative fantasy. These poor kids never knew whether I was telling the truth or telling a story, but this was the world as I dreamed it could be. Reconstructing some of my mother's or father's best stories, I could expand the tale into near reality while my big-eyed audience travelled with me from Africa to the Arctic! My obvious interests lent themselves to my credibility in this area of storytelling.

Beginning in junior high school, I was seldom without my briefcase full of research material on a scientific project. One Christmas, Mother ordered a good quality microscope from the Sears catalogue, which then became a most valuable tool in my self-education program. (Thank you, Mother.) This microscope was often carried around in my briefcase just in case a new and strange insect flew into my field of inspection or someone came to me with a question of *microscopic* significance.

Another source of credibility was the fact that in grade seven, I already owned my own homemade motorcycle and rode it to school. This sparked a lot of interest with the other boys, so that although my sports capabilities were a washout, I still had merit because of my understanding of machines. When my dad and I eventually built an aircraft and were out flying on the weekends, it gave me additional, interesting stories to talk about. These were a few of the saving factors of my childhood that allowed me to squeak through school without complete, apparent failure, at least in the eyes of my peers.

Am I really a dummy?

Academically, however, the results were not so encouraging. Lining up letters and numbers on paper, no matter how interesting the subject, just didn't seem to come natural. My teacher, in exasperation, would write on my report card, "Warren seems to understand the subject but is unable to demonstrate it on paper." Or another common remark was, "Warren seems to be smart enough if only he would apply himself." I thought to myself, "Well hello-o-o, does no one realize that *Warren* simply doesn't want to be here?"

Thanks to the many patient hours of reading with my mother, I entered junior high with above average reading abilities. This gave me a boost, because reading is most difficult for me to do. After my mom stopped reading with me at home, my skills dropped off until I finally ended up behind the rest of my class. I was struggling with concentration, struggling with staying on task and struggling with understanding how other people think.

Homework was difficult, as my parents were considerably less patient with me than my teachers. I was told over and over that folks would think I was a dummy if I couldn't do better than that. So, after ten years of continually hearing this, I learned to believe it. After all, it was obvious by my grades, right?

Those were years of extreme frustration and disappointment because even I believed I was smarter than this but was unable to somehow prove it. School continued to frustrate me until finally giving up in my second year through grade eleven. At that time, the outside world was loudly calling, and for me to complete grade 12 seemed improbable at best.

The dawn of understanding

I came away from school feeling defeated, but a clear understanding of why my mind worked so differently would not be revealed until years after joining the Royal Canadian Navy. I was trained as a Radar Plotter/Technician, which immersed me into all the Science one could hope for, and I was good at it. One of the main functions of my work was the actual plotting of contact information that we received from our ship's radars. The Plotter was required to write the information upside down and backwards on the plot, enabling the ship's Captain to read the information from the other side of the electronic table. This was a skill that came so naturally, that one time, while on a lonely night watch in the South Pacific, I discussed this phenomenon with my Watch Officer. He was quite interested in these strange abilities and suggested that I might have a condition known as "Dyslexia." This was an intriguing concept that might explain why school was so difficult and why my short-term memory was so terribly untrustworthy.

Many years later, I did some research on the subject and found that indeed, I did have symptoms of Dyslexia. This realization came too late, not that it could have likely helped anyway, but at least there was now an explanation for my appearing as a dummy in school.

Almost two decades later, I discovered yet another use for my so-called learning disability. At age 39, I was offered the distinct challenge of raising two of my nephews from early childhood until they were grown. These boys also suffered some setbacks in school that were similar to my own experience, which helped explain my own pilgrimage in greater detail. I discovered that for unfair reasons, they suffered from Fetal Alcohol Syndrome as well as Attention Deficit Disorder. These are conditions that in no way diminish the intelligence of a person but do cause some difficulty in concentrating on detailed studies or deskwork. The inability to sit still and focus in the presence of external distraction is the main challenge of these conditions, and of course does not lend itself to long hours of indoor learning at school.

As I helped my boys through these challenges, memories of my own schoolroom frustrations returned to me. Now, after years of studying the subject, I am certain that Attention Deficit Disorder may have further complicated my own Dyslexic condition and prevented me from excelling academically. As with my own experience, my boys found that they could learn or do just about anything, so long as they were not confined to a classroom setting. Both Trevor and Chad are extremely capable and hard working individuals who have valuable gifts and abilities that will allow them to succeed despite the setback of their unfair beginning.

Determination is the virtue most needed in circumstances like this. Not understanding what the problem is and believing that you are a dummy, is however, difficult to overcome. Even now, after three successful careers, I still cringe at hearing someone being called that. This evokes a flashback of memories from my childhood when "you dummy" was often directed at me. This condescending term eventually destroys a child's ability to see himself as a worthwhile person, often for life. I sometimes wonder how some of the other *less than perfect* children that I went to school with made out in life; the little chubby girl that was cruelly labelled "fatso!" or the little kid with thick glasses that was teased with "four eyes!" Were they ever able to overcome the debilitating comments that doubtlessly damaged them for life?

Character reconstruction

The day that I determined in my mind to join the Navy was a most fortunate turn of events. I had no idea what to expect, but soon found myself in an extremely beneficial training program that would change my life. After a five day train ride across our great nation, and upon disembarking the Queen of Arcadia onto the shores of beautiful Nova Scotia, we entered a whole new world. Several of us prairie boys who had joined up together found ourselves immersed in a veritable dismantling process that was designed to disassemble our old self-esteem and rebuild us from our character on up (for Queen and country, of course). It was a bit unnerving at the time, as our trainers would not let us cling to any of our old false securities, but planted instead, new reasons to live, develop, and feel good about oneself. Thus, much of our character that had been poorly formed or damaged in the past was rebuilt into a new and stronger disposition. Basic training at CFB Cornwallis was a nightmare for many men who refused to change, but for guys like me who did not like themselves anyway, it was a wonderful, growing experience.

Benefiting from a dyslexic mind

The principles learned as a child growing up on the farm with loving, responsible parents, coupled with the personal disciplines acquired from military training, formed a winning combination that allowed me to overcome many difficulties. I went on to enjoy nearly ten years of service with the RCN, serving on two Canadian destroyers and then as an Air Controller at Maritime Pacific Headquarters Operations (MarPac Ops). Following that, I served an additional twelve years with the Government of British Columbia as a Provincial Parks Ranger. The most enjoyable vocation I pursued was that of building my own businesses, followed by an additional thirteen years with the Alberta Government, managing park maintenance and operations.

The one notable thing that characterized each career was that very quickly, my supervisors realized that I could work very well on my own. Being dyslexic makes working with others in close situations difficult, but more importantly, develops a mind that can work even better, independently. Furthermore, my mind and heart seemed to have the natural ability to discern the gifts and abilities of others and being capable of managing people fairly and efficiently.

These were the positive results of what began as a devastating handicap, misunderstood by my teachers and parents. Today, looking back, I see that for every apparent disability we might have, we can also find within us a positive gift to compensate for it. If you have suffered from a setback such as this, may the following words be of encouragement to you.

Capitalize on your positive gifts and understand that you are not a dummy. You were simply created a little different. You are not below average, you are above average. You are not a failure, you're a winner, and if someone calls you a dummy, that makes them a liar. You are *not* a dummy, you are simply misunderstood.

Just remember confidently that, "God doesn't make any junk!" and walk away. If you have difficulty being understood by other people, then make the library your favourite place to hang out. Read all the good books you can in spite of how slowly you read. Why? Because one day, those people who think you are dumb may well be working for you! (Just smile.)

Finally, remember that it is not what you *do* in life but how you live your life that matters most! The Hollywood model of striving for riches and popularity is a formula for disappointment. The real blueprint for the success and happiness that we all hope for is found in using our personal gifts and talents in a way that will not only benefit us but others also.

230

Chapter
Ten

When the blind lead the blind

A culturally diverse land

As I was growing up in this culturally diverse land, my worldview developed as one of racial acceptance. I grew up with French neighbours on one side and Swedish on the other with Dutch and English right down the road. Within a five-mile radius of our northern home were Native Indians living next to Germans living next to Ukrainians and more. We all learned to appreciate one another's differences as we shared in the building of this new land.

Unfortunately, there were the inevitable exceptions. Occasionally, certain intolerant people ignorantly believed that one's worth differed with their skin colour or racial origin. This, I discovered to be rare but it nonetheless slithered into conversations from time to time.

The more obvious expression of this type of ignorance came in the form of religious discrimination. Because there were a large number of Catholic people in the area, our school was noticeably divided between the Catholic children and everybody else. The "everybody else" category was labelled Protestants, although many of the so-called Protestant kids didn't follow any recognizable faith. We fell into that category, rather by virtue of the fact that we were simply not Catholic. For most of the Protestant kids, our beliefs were simple; everyone had equal value as a citizen of this country (even if we didn't understand the difference between religions).

Only out on the playing field were people's true thoughts exposed. That's where I learned that I was going to hell and there would be no escape, not such a comforting feeling for a youngster surrounded by my accusers. At any rate, down deep we all knew that this couldn't really be true, at least we hoped it wasn't, because after all, if God made all children, why would He make some equal and some not?

These were the simple realities of growing up in such a religious and culturally diverse community. Most of our Catholic friends were very nice people and quite tolerant of our *religious ignorance*. It was only a select few on both sides of the fence that perpetuated discord amongst neighbours. I believe that this select few became responsible for the complete rejection of any religion that some people, like my parents, endorsed. Consequently, my parents were not exactly helpful when discussing religious matters. They were neither hot nor cold on the subject, so I assumed that they didn't know enough to give a definitive answer. When the topic was introduced, I often had to settle for a wave of their hand, which meant that the discussion was over. Obviously, in their minds, religion was so foolish a topic that it didn't warrant discussion.

A close encounter with the invisible

By the time I was ten years old, there were several churches thriving in the area, one of which was the United Church. At this church was a young student minister who came to preside over the congregation each summer. One year, he began a Boy's Club, which I attended and where I learned my first Bible memory verses. Here, I heard again some of the familiar Bible stories that Mother read to me when I was very young. The Boy's Club went on hikes along the Peace River and day trips around our farming community and generally had a good time together. I joined the Club, not because my parents were in favour of me learning any religion so much as in seeing me develop my interpersonal skills.

The one notable memory from that year was centred on a Bible verse we were asked to memorize. In John, chapter 14, verse one, Jesus is talking:

"Let not your heart be troubled, you believe in God, believe also in Me. In My Father's house are many mansions; if it were not so, I would have told you, for I go to prepare a place for you. And if I go and prepare a place for you, I will come again and receive you to Myself; that where I am, there you may be also."

This seemingly innocent verse of Scripture somehow made a deep impression upon me. At least it seemed that way, because while I was pondering the possibilities of this Scripture, the thoughts virtually flooded in as feelings. This was a different concept for me, because, like everyone else, I was used to assessing conceptions only with my mind. This, then, made me take notice at the time.

Upon questioning my parents about this phenomenon, I was met with ridicule and criticism. My father was a professing atheist while my mother, who was at least aware of the good that the Church could do in people's lives, was very critical. Discussion was not proving to be very productive in this area so I dropped the issue at home and pondered all these possibilities within myself.

Several days later, while walking along the road near our farm and talking to myself out loud (for lack of better company) about the Scripture that I had memorized, something happened that I should never forget. As I was pondering all these confusing feelings that seemed to be welling up in me, I became acutely aware of a presence nearby. Stopping and trying to see what this was on that August summer day, I found myself strangely aware that I should be afraid, when in fact, the reverse was the case. Whatever this was became as real as anything in my visual sight, but again, strangely, it was not visible with my eyes. So, although I could see the road, the fence, trees and the nearby field with my eyes, here was something, or possibly someone that was just as real but was not visible. Very strange! As I stood there blinking, trying to see what this thing was, a conversation occurred that was quite warming.

The detailed memory of that conversation has all but faded from me, although I clearly remember that I had been spoken to and as far as I know was able to answer back. What or exactly who spoke was a mystery to me and I puzzled over it for a long time afterward. Whatever the conversation was that took place at that moment left me without any doubt that a real world existed outside of my third dimensional awareness. Coming away from that experience left me excited, but certain that this would not be something that I could discuss with my father.

Awareness of the paranormal

I found myself feeling somehow different, although visibly the same. The conversation that "we" had there in secret gave me a very present and uncommon peace and insight that wasn't in me before. It was so indelibly profound an experience that no one would ever convince me that this incident never really happened.

After that occurrence, everything supernatural or paranormal in my reading became infinitely more interesting. The school library had become my favourite haunt, which was not only a great place to hide, but provided me with a new dimension of learning and growth. Religion, however, because of my father's leading, was something that I would continue to avoid at all costs. My mother would sit quietly while Dad ranted on about some of the religious people who came to visit. I always thought that they seemed nice enough, but if Dad thought that they were bad, then I supposed they should be avoided. He seemed to simply enjoy a good debate with these people, and over the years he gained lots of practice. Having listened to my father dominate so many religious discussions with ridicule eventually made me good at avoiding religion and also able to argue the so-called facts.

Humour from the pulpit

There came a day, however, that my mother decided that it would be good for us all to get some religious culture (likely encouraged by our church going friends). She convinced us all to attend the little United Church on Sundays. This obviously brought about a long list of complaints from Dad and us kids, but we went anyway and even enjoyed it most of the time.

236

One Sunday, the preacher was hammering away at us poor sinners, when some mischievous fellow outside began tearing around with his motorcycle. The motorcyclist rode around and around the block making extra revving sounds as he came by the church. Just as the preacher was getting to a significant point in the sermon, this loud old Norton motorbike would roar by. I remember all the boys craning their necks to catch a glimpse of the bike out of the church windows. The insolent biker made several noisy trips around the block, being as disturbing as he possibly could. Finally, with the preacher almost screaming over the sound, the bike roared by one fast and final time.

As it came to the corner adjacent to the church, there was a sudden crash, the sound of metal sliding on gravel and then a dreadful silence. The preacher stopped for a moment and peered out the window at the biker who was trying to pry himself from under his dusty old bent up bike. When our minister came back to the pulpit, he said in a quiet and sheepish voice, "Thank God for answered prayer!" The kids all looked at each other in amazement. Wow! Was there really a God who could do that? We grinned at the thought of God having such a great sense of humour!

Tuned in to the wrong god

That summer, the Catholic Church in our town was damaged by fire. The United Church student minister at the time did what every good Christian should do and invited the whole Catholic congregation to hold their mass along with our Sunday service. Now, here was something that impressed my folks. I heard from several people that "this is how it should be done" and that there shouldn't be all these differences in churches if there was only one God anyway. What great meetings they were, with all of us crammed together in that little Church for worship services. Sunday after Sunday, we came together where our preacher and the Catholic Father would share the service. Afterward, the men all stood outside and smoked and spit and talked about the state of the crops, while the women exchanged stories and chatted about children. For the first time, Protestant and Catholic kids played together feeling *almost* equal.

This went on successfully for a few weeks, as I recall, until the United Church circuit preacher came by to bolster the work of the young student minister. That particular Sunday, the student minister sat in the front pew with the rest of us while the seasoned circuit minister delivered the message. I will always recall that the student was much more interesting and seemingly much more in tune with the people. But none the less, the senior guy surely thought he was something special as he delivered a stern message that Sunday with the utmost of enthusiasm. Unfortunately, while he held the pulpit and everyone's attention, he made good his chance to deliver a stinging blow to our Catholic friends and neighbours. By the time he had finished explaining that it was the Catholics who were hopelessly bound for hell, there was noticeably more room in the church, though the air was strangely hotter.

Cars left in a spray of gravel as others stomped out and walked home. Only a few of the original United Church members stayed, along with the young upstart minister who sat in the front pew with his head in his hands. After the circuit minister shook hands with the last of the congregation, he left and so did we. It had taken only one man, obviously in tune with the wrong god, to destroy what was developing into a notable ministry. That minister may have come back again, but a part of the church body never returned, and we were among them.

Avoiding religion at any cost

At the time, that seemed to solidify yet another reason to avoid religion altogether, because I wondered how two ministers who were both reading the same Book could be so different in their views. I guess we see that kind of thing in every area of life, though, where some people are genuine and some are complete fakes. Unfortunately, some of the fakes hold offices of authority and great trust, as did that circuit preacher!

As a child, the one thing I did learn about religion was that the people in my hometown who were Christians were never perceived as crooked in any way. One could always trust them and rely on them, which seemed to me to be a compelling reason to join them rather than shun them. But, my father was strong in his argument and compelling in his own way where I was concerned. Dad never actually gave me instruction to keep clear of religious people. His only influence was that of verbal distaste for their beliefs that I thought best not to challenge.

When I was eighteen, I made a break from farm life and the country that I loved so much, leaving for my first Naval posting to Canadian Forces Base Cornwallis. This was situated along the Bay of Fundy near Digby, Nova Scotia. Here, we were near the beautiful Annapolis Valley, which was a real treat for those of us who were *western boys*. In June of 1968, the Valley was decorated with the blossoms of a million fruit trees and the rich green of the Nova Scotia countryside. I spent nine gruelling weeks here in training and grew to love the beauty of the area.

Upon completing Basic Training in Cornwallis and Trades Training in Halifax, the Navy offered me a posting to Her Majesty's Canadian Ship (H.M.C.S.) St. Croix on the west coast of Canada. Leaving Halifax in the cold of December and riding the rails across the country for six days, I arrived in balmy Vancouver where the weather was warm and the grass was still green. On the bus trip to Victoria, I would enjoy my second ferry ride ever, as it crossed over the Strait of Georgia. Victoria was the most beautiful place I had ever seen, and although I couldn't yet know it, Vancouver Island would be my home for the next nineteen years.

Sailing into sin and debauchery

I very much enjoyed my Navy career, sailing around the Pacific and visiting exotic South Sea places. As my career expanded, there were, unfortunately, many opportunities to become entangled in serious and wicked activities.

For instance, while visiting Wellington, New Zealand in 1969, there were times that I found myself sickened by what I saw in the nightclubs of that busy metropolis. Many of the other fellows indulged in the so-called fun and the booze, but for some reason, I found that I did not share their enthusiasm. I wasn't sure why I felt so different than my shipmates, and had to endure their sickening stories when they finally staggered back to the ship. Possibly, I was just cut from a different cloth, or perhaps my country background had taught me to hate these filthy parts of the world. At any rate, I knew this was not for me. The overseas lands that we visited were very enjoyable. The common people were friendly but it was the filthy parts of the cities that I couldn't bare. My favourite poet, Robert Service, in his depiction of the first cities in the Yukon, called them "plague spots" and I was now beginning to realize that these were often accurate depictions of certain areas of many cities around the world.

It was then that my preoccupation with flying became so useful, being a gyrocopter pilot, a member of the Victoria Flying Club and the Popular Rotorcraft Association. Whenever we arrived at a new port, I went ashore ready and armed with names and addresses of club members in the area. As my shipmates went off to compete for "Pig of the Month" in the downtown brothels of Auckland or Sidney or Brisbane, I was off to find new flying friends outside of the city.

Without exception I came home having had a great time with wonderful flying pictures to prove my stories. I also met some of the most gorgeous bronzen girls while out flying and exploring and was thankful that these were not the kind I had noticed in some bars.

Checking out an Australian gyrocopter

A strange turn of events

Years went by, and eventually I met a pretty lady of my own back in Victoria, B.C. We married and began to build a family there in the Garden City.

During my third year of marriage, and upon completion of my pay level three Radar and A.S.W. (anti-submarine warfare) training at Fleet School, something very puzzling took place. Many of us were once again waiting for a draft to active duty on a Canadian destroyer. Then, on the day my draft was handed to me, I nearly cried. They had posted me to the main gate of Naden! This was the Navy land base of C.F.B Esquimalt and not on a ship! What was going on here? I had been trained as a Marine Radar Plotter and extensively in anti-submarine warfare! This should never have happened!

In days to come, as this disgruntled sailor reluctantly checked entrance passes and ID cards at the main gate, another puzzled young man whose name was Dick was drafted in to help me. Now, Dick was as disenchanted as I was about the draft. He had just finished his Level Three training as a Marine Engineer and was dreaming of an edifying draft to H.M.C.S Provider. This was most certainly a confusing turn of events for the both of us, but for the next several weeks we shared gate duties at Naden.

Dick and I would alternate for an hour on the gate, checking car passes and then an hour in the office checking pedestrians and answering phones. It wasn't a difficult job; all we had to do was make sure we didn't let in any Russian armoured tanks or strange men with long hair!

Dick proved to be a great source of entertainment during those weeks, as he was a staunch Brethren churchman and quite verbal about his faith. I was up to the task in fine form, however, and with my old arguments polished to perfection, we engaged in, well - - - let's call them *discussions*. At least we didn't raise our voices (much) as we probed through that ancient book they call the Bible. Dick was good, I'll give him that. I'm not sure how my father would have handled it but I felt that I would have "done him proud" with my arguments.

Day after day, night shift after night shift, we battled reason with what I called an antiquated book. Dick would read some of the Scriptures to me and then leave me to defend myself as the consummate sinner that I was. Throughout those weeks of enjoying our landlocked battle zone, we became great friends and verbal sparring partners.

Suddenly lacking the necessary resources

On a quiet August evening, Dick and I were again sharing a shift together on base. Our polarized dialogue continued as before. "Come on," I said wearily, "I'm a good enough guy, why would I need to be *saved* from anything; I never killed anyone or have stolen anything (at least not very expensive). Look, I live a good life; I am a good family man with a good job, what could be wrong?" "Well, you have life all figured out, don't you?" he said. "But life is the easy part. What about death? Do you have that taken care of?" (Oops, now I was in trouble.)

"The wisest man in the world reminded us that we have no power in the hour of our death and we have no ability to hold back our spirit when we die," said Dick. "So, now what are you going to do? Do you know where you are going? I mean, for sure! Don't you understand that the God who gave us life also has the power to take care of us beyond death? I'm sure that your father didn't show you what to do about life after death, did he? No, he only argued why you shouldn't follow good people, right? What kind of sense does that make? Don't forget, it wasn't your dad, but Jesus who said 'Follow me', and it was Jesus who assured us that 'He is the way, the truth and the life and that He is the only hope of getting beyond this life to meet God.' All we need to do is believe in God's plan to pay for our

244

sins by the death of His own Son. We certainly can't afford to pay for our own sins," Dick reminded me. "No one has the necessary resources for that." (My argument began to lack the necessary research at this moment. And I wondered what Dad would have said here.)

Dick reminded me that when Jesus left the earth, He went to finish building a new world that would replace this one when it was finally destroyed by fire. (I'd heard that somewhere before.) He went on to say that every person in this world is going to be subject to the fate of this world, which would mean destruction by fire. (Now let's be serious here, I figured.) In my *let's get real* tone of voice, I stated, "What kind of a God would do such a thing as that!"

There was a moment of silence and then he responded with a steady tone of voice. "Only the God who loves us so much that he risked sending his Son to this dying planet to bail us out! Only the God who has given up the life of his own Son to rescue us from a world dominated by evil. He is the one whom you have laughed at and used his name for a curse word, the one who is offering a way for us to get off this sorry planet before it burns! If we reject such a great sacrifice and gift, do you think He won't be disappointed and even angry?"

Oh boy, now I've done it

Dick also said that this God calls each of us by knocking at the door of our conscience, hopeful that we will respond and invite Him into our life.

"All He wants is our friendship," he said, "so invite him in and ask forgiveness for all the things you knew you did wrong in life. God does say, 'For every one that asks, receives; and he that seeks, finds; and to him that knocks, it shall be opened.'" (Are you kidding, I thought, ask forgiveness... for ALL my sins! Oh boy, that could take a long time and besides, who wants to be religious!) Then, as if he knew my thoughts, Dick said, "When you get a chance, read the first four books of the New Testament. You will find that the very last thing God desires for man is religion." I retorted, "I still don't see why we should even need a god from some other place. It is just a crutch, I think, and I don't need a crutch because life is fine just the way it is."

My friend patiently continued. "Long ago, humans got away from the perfection that they were designed with. They allowed sin to become a part of them. Sin is like a disease; only it is an ailment we are now all born with that prevents us from living a healthy, spiritual and physical life the way God intended for us. God says again, 'There is none righteous, not even one.' This sin sickness cannot be treated in the body, nor can it be cleansed away by anything that we do for ourselves. Because it is a spiritual disease, we must treat it in the spiritual realm, which is where God lives. Though it seems strange for us now in this physical dimension, Jesus has become our prescription. Sin is like drunkenness; the more we indulge, the less we are aware that we have a problem. Christ's death created a kind of spiritual medicine that we need to reach out and ask for, to cleanse us of the disease of our sin."

I pondered those things for a while. When we changed shift positions again, I stayed down at the gate with

Dick instead of going up to the warm office. Dick went on now in the freedom of my pondering silence. "Once we have invited this gift, the Son of God (Jesus) into our lives, we should then try to live a life worthy of that gift. It is the gift of eternal life that we receive from God when we believe in Jesus as the Son of God. When we ask for forgiveness with the hope that He will help us stay clean, that's called repentance," he told me. "The realization of the fact that Christ actually is the Son of God and that He really did allow Himself to be killed in our place is what will set you free from the disease of sin," he explained.

An element of fearful truth

Now, I'm not dumb, and I really did believe that there was a God. I also found no reason to dispute the fact that his Son was called Jesus. So, I began to ponder how a being as powerful as God would allow his own Son to be butchered for men. Especially some of the men I know! Somehow, there was an element of fearful truth beyond the fun of the debate we were having. Dick told me then that the time we live in is considered the "end times" and we are to expect to hear a trumpet blow and Jesus will return to pick up those believers who have not yet died and gone on to heaven. I was becoming less and less argumentative as a deep comprehension came over me.

If this story had even a tiny shred of truth to it, I was well deserving of the fire reserved for the likes of me, even though I had considered myself a good person by contrast. While in my quiet assessment of the matter, Dick said, "Consider the symbol for Christianity, the cross. It is an *empty* cross, right? The greatest news is that, unlike every other religious leader on earth, Jesus rose from the dead!" (This was different; I hadn't considered that aspect of the story before.) If this Jesus was really alive and I could really know him, then this is better than religion, I surmised!

"That," smiled my friend, "is the part about Christianity that I like the most. Not only did He provide a cleansing for the things we do wrong in our lives, but He also promises to live with us and help us here while we are still on the earth." I looked at him in disbelief! "You mean that those Christian people I laughed at all those years actually 'walk and talk' with God! And all the while I was teasing them and arguing with them, they actually *did* have eternal life?"

"Yes", Dick told me, and then went on. "We have the freedom to say no to Jesus, of course, but you must understand that the wrath of God is then justified when we choose to live in our sin rather than taking the free gift he offered us." I agreed, thinking of what it would mean to give up one of my own beautiful little daughters for someone else's wrongdoing and then have them refuse the sacrifice I had made for them!

I suddenly felt a need to talk to this God. I left the gate, feeling as though He might be descending on the planet any minute to call His people home. Jumping over the swing gate in the office, I dove for the privacy of the furnace room. As of now, all the foolish arguments that I had learned from my father seemed so shallow and meaningless. I finally understood that this was not just a story; it was in fact a reality.

My second close encounter

For the first time in my 25-year-life, I could see the difference between what I knew of religion and the reality of a warm relationship that God was offering me now. I had read a lot about the religions of the world and had wondered what small minds it must have taken to worship a big green stone god, some foolish idol or an impersonal, mystical presence. I knew that I was stronger and smarter than that. And I also knew that every other god that I had studied was dead.

But, here I was, even on my knees, with tears flowing and heart pounding, begging God not to pass me over but to forgive me of all the things that I had done in my life that displeased Him. He suddenly became so real, and I invited Him in to me, not knowing what would happen next. Everything was quiet. "There must be more to this," I thought, so I asked God for forgiveness again and invited Him in again. Fortunately, no one came through my office at the main gate at that moment. My whole being was alive with a sensation that something had happened, but it was completely unexplainable with my limited, human thinking. There were no lightning bolts or thundering voices at the time, but I was keenly aware of God's presence, a friendly, powerful presence that I somehow recognized.

Off shift, I felt a great peace within me and just knew something was different. I longed for a moment with God himself. Driving up to the top of Mount Doug that night, I sat high up on a rock looking down over the city of Victoria and again renewed my request. For a

249

long while, I just thought the whole plan over. I had done it! I had actually done what I figured would never happen! I gave my life (foolish as it seemed) to God Himself, and not only that, but I felt good about it. There was a wonderful sense of peace within me, that I had done something very right.

I felt like a new person that night. I know that my dad would laugh at me if I used the word 'born again' because he couldn't possibly understand what happens between the powerful Being who constructed the whole universe and some feeble, foolish human. Nor could he ever understand the fabulous feeling of finally understanding what the life of Jesus was all about. High up on that mountain under the stars, I just laid there as though wrapped in God's great, loving arms and enjoyed my newly found peace.

Strangely, only a few days after this, both Dick and I were transferred out to our ships. Whenever we both arrived back in port at the same time, Dick would invite me to hang out with him and study the Bible. Over the months that followed, I went to church (can you imagine me going to church!) several times with my friend and began to gain a better understanding of what the Bible *really* says.

All I had previously known of the Bible was of no use because I now found that so little of what my father said about religion had been correct. Now, I was finding out that this was the most interesting book I had ever picked up and that it was full of wonderful wisdom. Here, I found concepts that I had needed my whole life to help me understand other people as well as the world around me. I also discovered that this was unlike any other religion that I had read about.

250

Most religions had one great prophet or leader who wrote the book on that particular faith. Virtually all religions I had read about either believed in a god that had once lived but had died and ceased to exist, or that the whole cosmos was a god. I found that type of thinking to be insulting to my intelligence. But, here was I, alive and actually walking and talking with the Creator of the entire universe! To top that, "He" was interested in me!

My friendship with God has now lasted over thirty years and it only seems to get better and more intimate. When I first became a Christian I expected to discover what most of the world is suspicious about, that God is really a hard task master, distant and somewhat cold. But, I am thankful to report that the opposite is true. Unlike other so-called gods in this world who demand our children as sacrifice to them in some way, here is the creator God who offered His only Son as a sacrifice for us!

Over the years, I have walked and talked with God and have experienced His presence as gentle and loving in every area of life. These days, I go off to sleep discussing the day with my friend Jesus, and awaken in the morning aware of His presence in me, and being able to ask for a daily supply of wisdom and strength.

I now know that it was God that I had encountered on that dirt road back in August of 1960. He must have spoken directly to my spirit and changed me enough to keep me from being destroyed in the gutters of this world. Being an ardent explorer and adventurer, there was always the danger of wandering into something beyond my ability to escape. Actually, I believe that He gave me a sense of this danger and supplied the way to escape it. The world is full of traps for those who have no sense, snares such as drugs and booze, wild living or the occult.

I won't tell you that life has been easy since inviting Jesus in -- an adventure, yes, sometimes difficult, yes, but every single day, God has been there for me, for which I am very thankful.

Just enough room in this old Cessna 172 for the pilot and five crazy jumpers

For a few years, I belonged to the Canadian Sport Parachuting Association. Jumping out of a Cessna 172 was a great experience and a definite adrenaline rush! As I discovered later in life, this had been a good parallel to my being able to understand how to live the Christian life. Despite the bulkiness of the chute that I wore skydiving, it gave me a wonderful sense of

252

security and peace when I had it on. Much like that parachute, my relationship with Christ provides the security required for the *life beyond*, as well as any danger I might encounter in this life. Years spent adventuring in this way was extreme fun and I met a number of nice people *up there*. I used to save all my extra cash in order to make two or three jumps on a sunny Saturday. We would all assemble at the Flight Centre at Victoria International Airport and pack our chutes in readiness for the next flight up. Five of us young fun seekers would cram into that little airplane with our bulky parachutes. There were no seats for the jumpers so we crawled in and rested on our knees with our chutes against the back wall of the cockpit. The pilot would then radio the tower and head out to the main runway on half flat tires that begged for a lighter load. With the engine howling at full power, we would labour into the air and slowly climb out over the beautiful Saanich Peninsula to where our drop zone was located.

The jumpers were so packed in, that with the door closed there wasn't enough room to make a decision! The parachute packs were bulky and uncomfortable but we gladly wore them, knowing the vicarious nature of our intentions up there.

Having arrived over the drop zone, the jumpmaster would open the right hand door and lock it up under the wing, then help to manoeuvre the first person out and get them away. Sequentially, each of us then took our turn crawling on hands and knees to the door, preparing to make an exhilarating exit. Once out of the door, we stood with our left foot on the wheel and hung onto the wing strut for dear life! Standing right behind that howling engine was windy and loud, but once we pushed off from that little piece of noisy security, everything became delightfully quiet. The chute would either open by a static line, fastened to the plane, or, as our skills increased, we could pull the ripcord and open the chute ourselves. The descent was made in wonderful silence, giving us a peaceful time before we had to brace ourselves for the landing. Looking back now at my daily relationship with Christ and having God's Spirit living in me, my days were much like skydiving, often so exhilarating that no external drugs were required to get the most out of life.

There were still periodic hard times when it was like landing in a crosswind and difficult to know what might happen next. Also, there is no doubt that this life takes guts and work, just as we had to work hard to be good at skydiving and careful not to make foolish decisions in the air.

Never go out without your parachute

Christianity is often like wearing the parachute itself. In order to be ready for anything each day, I make sure that my *chute* is in good shape and that I never take it off. In my relationship with my friend Jesus, I keep checking to make sure that I don't go places that He won't want to go. You might ask, "Don't you find it uncomfortable wearing your Christian parachute all the time?" and I will tell you, "Yes, sometimes it gets uncomfortable. This can happen in a setting where I find myself in ungodly company. On occasion, people will look at me like I'm wearing a parachute uptown, alright, and I feel a bit out of place. But, I know how important it is to maintain my relationship with God and that I am ready for anything at anytime because of it.

In the years following, I had many discussions with my parents about the validity of Christianity as opposed to the falsehood of religion. As expected, my parents countered me with the same old arguments that I knew they would use. A breakthrough came, however, in 1982, when, after pleading with God not to let my mother die without knowing Him, she too surrendered to Christ only days before her death.

Throughout that period, I found my father a calloused and hard opponent whenever religion was the topic. I prayed daily and did all in my power to love him even when he remained hard and unlovable. He came to live with me in the year 2000 and continued to be immovable in his thinking. As we gradually became more comfortable with one another, Father even witnessed some striking miracles first hand in our home, but was unable to reconcile his thinking. Finally, after spending a delightful Christmas at home with us in 2006, he entered the hospital in pain and failing health. We continued to pray for him and plead with the Author of Life for his salvation. On the 10th of January 2007, while Father and I were having a bedside discussion about life, he asked me about some of the tough questions he had regarding God and religion. As I prayerfully answered his questions, he finally put his great pride aside and surrendered to the Creator of all things, Christ the Lord. At that moment, the Bible tells us, the angels rejoiced and Dad's name was entered into the "Book of Life," sealing his salvation forever.

We live or die according to our choices

We all live and die by the choices we make in life. Each of us has the choice to follow rock stars, human philosophies or various religions. Sometimes, we even unquestioningly follow our parents' brand of religion or unbelief. On the day we stand before God, though, we cannot blame anyone else for the results of our decisions; they were, after all, <u>our</u> decisions. It is written, "If the blind lead the blind, both shall fall into a pit."

*** WHEN YOU'RE IN CONTROL ***

It's a great feeling
When you're at the helm,
With the wind in your favour
And the water so calm.

When you're in control
And the sailing is fine,
Reach out to Him
While there is still time.

For beyond the fog
In the thick misty cloud,
Disaster awaits you
If you stand too proud.

So call upon Him
While He is near,
Put your life in His hands
You'll have nothing to fear.

-- *Doug Greenfield*

Chapter Eleven

Shopping for a baby sister

Our terrible loss

Mother celebrated her thirty-fifth birthday on July 11th. 1954, just six days after Elvis made his debut somewhere far to the south of us. This year held great hope for our family as well, but was, however, destined to end in sorrow. Mother spent six long months convalescing with a difficult pregnancy that would end in gloomy disappointment by autumn.

That fall, my new baby sister was born premature and still, so there was great sorrow in our home. These days were so hard on Mom that I spent a great deal of time at our neighbours with Norman and Dolly Barnhardt. I had a good time with them, as I recall, but could not understand why the separation was necessary.

While travelling along in the pick-up truck with Mr. Barnhardt, one day, I reportedly suffered a sudden intense agricultural awareness. Standing up on the seat, I announced in my four-year-old voice, "God yes, Norman, oats and barley, oats and barley!" This story was circulated around the Project, as was a picture of me standing victorious over a dead yearling bear and holding a rifle that was considerably taller than I was. (I believe the marksman was actually Mr. Barnhardt who was no doubt defending his livestock.)

That summer, I also spent time with my little friend Laurie at the Barry family's home while my mother rested. Even as a four-year-old, I could sense the change in atmosphere in our home well before understanding the change in circumstances. The atmosphere was one of distress and confusion throughout that time. This led into a bitterly cold winter through which I recall my mother wanting to go back home to Saskatchewan. There were long and sometimes heated discussions about this, which resulted in a promise to make the trip back as soon as the business would allow.

By the time the migrating birds had once again returned to nest and the crop was planted, we began to make preparations for that long journey. Our '52 Chevy pickup truck, with its homemade canopy on the back would be our trusty transportation and our home away from home.

In late June, we hired Claude, a dependable young man from a neighbouring farm to care for our place while we were away. Claude was responsible for the critical job of milking the cows each morning and evening as well as feeding the pigs and poultry. He was also charged with weeding the garden and the completion of forty acres of summer ploughing.

Dad left young Claude with these four simple instructions..."Be sure to feed the animals and milk the cows regularly, finish the ploughing, keep the weeds out of the garden and whatever you do, don't swim in the dugout."

The cutest baby on the ward

With that, we were off on a new adventure to see a faraway world called Saskatchewan. After a long, dusty trip to Edmonton, I became aware of an exciting part of this plan that was a definite surprise to me. We visited the paediatric ward of an enormous hospital, where, to my great excitement, we got to choose a new baby sister! This seemed inconceivable and was kind of like shopping for a little sister in a baby supermarket! After some deliberation, my parents made their decision for adoption. Seemingly, the final choice was based on the simple fact that their chosen baby was without argument the cutest baby on the ward. There may have been other considerations but I recall that this one characteristic was most talked about. We made plans to claim baby Sylvia on our way back from Saskatchewan and then headed out with renewed joy for our trip ahead.

A faraway world called Saskatchewan

Upon arriving in Govan, Saskatchewan, I discovered an endless supply of cousins that I had never met before. I don't recall being able to master all of their names, as they were older and far bolder, and virtually ran over top of me at the time. As a shy five year old from the bush, this was a daily challenge until becoming more familiar with my strange and busy surroundings.

It was 1955, and while, on the radio, the Dominos were singing, "I'll Never Get to Heaven," the farmers in Saskatchewan were crying, "I'll never get my crop off!" It was a wet year for those farmers and there were many flooded fields. In some places, only the narrow road allowance protruded through the middle of some of these recent *lakes*. For kids, however, it was great because we got to go swimming in the deep sloughs and ditches!

Grandmother Hampton's house out on the farm was a grand structure for the day and I am sure it cost Grandpa more than he could have anticipated. What a contrast from our cabin in the north, was this great house. It had a vast kitchen with pantry, a dining area and parlour larger than I had ever seen. There was a great, dark cellar below and a long, elegant stairway that led to the upstairs bedrooms. My mom proudly showed me all the places where she used to play as a

261

child. She reminisced about all her favourite childhood pleasures and then led me up yet another dark stairway to the old creaky attic, which left me light headed and frightened.

Grandmother and Grandfather Hampton had planted trees to shade the yard (a rare commodity for that area) and real lawn for kids to play on. This was quite a novelty because up until that time, grass, in my experience was only for cows to eat. (Actually, come to think of it, I still feel that way about lawns.)

For my mother and dad, this was a long, overdue reprieve. They were able to visit with many friends and family, catch up on all the news and just enjoy being back home again. It was good to see their brothers and sisters and to see how each of their lives and families were taking shape. It was also a time to reflect on their decision to homestead so far away in the north, and at the last, it seemed to refuel their desire to continue that dream.

Finally, the day came to depart for the north once again. After tears and hugs, we soon headed back on the long road home. Since the prairie highways were not well developed, flooding had caused widespread disaster for travellers. This resulted in our having to drive all the way to the U.S. border to get back into Alberta.

The mystery of the disappearing farm hand

In a few days, we were back in Edmonton and visiting more relatives and friends. Everyone was excited about our new baby, so we had great support the day we arrived to pick up our chosen little bundle of joy.

My new little sister had, of course, only known the warmth and consistency of the hospital, so nothing on earth could have prepared her for the trip and the life she was about to embark upon. From the fourth floor of a modern hospital to our little home in the bush would be a shocking experience that would upset anyone and would qualify her as a true, pioneer baby.

We started out on that long 300-mile dirt road journey with excitement in our hearts, looking forward to getting back home again. The roads were predictably horrible, causing a rash of flat tires along the way. Then, to add to the experience, with each flat tire, little Sylvia donated a messy diaper to enhance the moment. This became a memorable and much talked about trip for years to come.

If the trip home had not been stressful enough for my parents, what was waiting when they arrived back would surely exceed all mysteries. As we drove into the farmyard, it was quite evident that the garden had received little or no care while we were gone. Then, as we climbed down from the truck, we could hear the cattle, bawling frantically in the barn. A worried expression came across Dad's face and he headed on the run toward the barn. Mom went into the house to get baby Sylvia settled and I stood at the gate to the barnyard, watching my dad run back and forth, feeding hungry, penned up animals. To Father's disgust, he found that the cows had been locked in the barn for at least a week without feed or water and were at the stage of frenzied panic.

Hungry pigs and chickens had eaten everything in sight in the confines of their pens and were also out of water. Dad got back to the house in the cool of the evening, tired and disgusted with the whole situation.

"Have you seen that good for nothing Claude?" he growled. "No," Mom said, "and you know, Frank, it is strange, but all of the new baby bottles that I bought before we left home are missing!" "I'm not surprised," said Dad, leaning on the counter. "There is a rope tied across the dugout, which means he was swimming in our drinking water, and...the @#%**# tractor is missing!"

Poor little Sylvia had to make do with only a half-sized bottle for a while until we could purchase some new full-sized ones again. Dad finally found the tractor, stuck in the bush at the end of the field with the plough still attached. The seat was missing and the engine had only quit when it ran out of fuel. With the garden high in weeds, the animals hungry and thirsty, the tractor in the bush and all the new baby bottles missing, the big question was, "Where in the world was Claude?"

Within a few days, we had all the answers and as the story unfolded, the intensity of my parents' anger diminished, replaced instead by the rib tickling humour of the truth.

You see, Claude was a typical, fun loving, impulsive young man. On the Friday after we had left on our trip, he was dutifully working on his 40-acre ploughing project, bouncing on the seat of the old Minneapolis tractor and singing at the top of his lungs. What could be more enjoyable, out in the fresh sweet air, enjoying the warm summer breezes? Basking in the moment, he was feeling good about the responsibility that had been entrusted to him. Sadly, a moment was all he had before the spring seat snapped and plummeted Claude over the back of the tractor and through the plough! Now, with multiple bruises and wounded pride, he dug himself out of the dirt as the tractor roared away. Claude's sense of joy and song vanished like the morning dew as he limped back to the house.

There was a dance in town that Saturday night, and Claude, needing some stress relief, made plans to attend. After evening chores, he left the cattle in the barn so that he would not have to round them up the following morning for milking. Now, Claude wasn't old enough to buy liquor to take to the dance, so he searched our house for a way to smuggle out some of Mother's dandelion wine. To his delight, he found the perfect containers. Yes, there were little Sylvia's new baby bottles, and who would suspect? With each bottle filled and capped, he could smuggle his booty into the dance and enjoy the evening.

Now, he may have pulled it off had he not decided to show his visiting cousin how the "big boys" in Alberta could party. As the evening diminished, so did the wine until the lads lost all track of time. By the time the stars were out and all the sensible animals had gone to bed, the R.C.M.P arrived on their community patrol to check on the dance. I doubt that it would have taken much of a detective to determine that a youth his age was having way too much fun! The duty officer opened Claude's car door just as he was enjoying a swig from the baby bottle. Only a momentary search was required to give the Mounties all the evidence they needed to escort the embarrassed young man off to the slammer in Spirit River. Gone were the new baby bottles, gone was our trusty caretaker and gone once again was Claude's moment of bliss.

After we arrived home, it took quite some time for the cows to resume full milk capacity, because consistent milk production depends upon regular milking twice a day. It also depends upon a good feed and water supply that had been denied them for a period of time. The tractor was refuelled and the seat repaired without too much difficulty, but it took a good long time to weed the garden and nurse the stock back to full health.

Angelic presence

With that series of adventures, baby Sylvia arrived on the farm and took up residence as the *Queen of the House*. Then began our newest learning curve. Feed baby Syl, tuck her in, stroke her cute little face and whisper, "Nite, nite." Close the door quietly, and before you could tip toe to your cold cup of coffee, the bottle would hit the floor with a crash! Open the door and there would be baby Syl, jumping up and down in her crib with a great big smile on her face. She wasn't a bad baby; no, not at all, she was simply born a consummate socialite.

If there is one depiction that would characterize that child, it was that she needed constant company every hour of every day, even in the hours that my poor mom was hoping to get some sleep. So it was, that as Buddy Holly released his new record, "Baby, Let's Play

House," Mother was weeping, "Baby, let's get some sleep!"

My little sister grew fast and made an indelible impression on everyone she came in contact with. Here was a little girl with such charm and angelic presence that she captured the hearts of all. I waited patiently for the little playmate that I hoped she could some day be. Sylvia seemed oblivious to the fact that I was waiting for her to *hurry up and grow*. She lay on her blanket and cooed, gurgled and played with no apparent awareness of the panic I was in to have her join me in my world. Regularly, we lay side by side and attempted to play together which inevitably ended with me in tears. What was wrong here? I had learned to understand every other creature in my world, so why was it so hard, I wondered, to understand this new little person?

Stay away from the sharp end!

Each time I tried to hold this little smiling angel and offer her some love, she would bite me! There was no convincing my mother to put a muzzle on her, and since there isn't a S.P.C.B. (Society for the Prevention of Cruelty to Brothers) I had to endure and learn to *stay away from the sharp end!*

My little sister became a roving explorer as she learned to crawl and the whole house was at risk. If all was quiet and Sylvia was not in sight, one could be certain that there was soon to be a great calamity or one of our pets might be in grave danger. She had an uncanny ability to stealthily approach when you were not watching and inflict a severe bite to your

267

unsuspecting backside. Some of these attacks even left marks! Immediately after the dastardly deed was done, my darling little sister would sit happily down with the most adorable look of satisfaction, and beam angelically. This tactic made tattling a near impossibility, so my sweet little sister would triumph once again.

Sylvia never did learn to appreciate the great outdoors with me, although we did eventually learn to play board games together, *safely*. This whole experience gave me training that would last a lifetime. One learned to quickly survey every room being entered, looking for pending danger. Once danger is detected and its movement plotted, you must quickly pre-plan an escape route. The operative word here is *quickly*, which, for me took several painful attempts to perfect.

There were, however, definite advantages to having a small person like her who found it utterly impossible to be still. With Sylvia racing about the house like a whirlwind and climbing on virtually every accessible shelf or table, Mom did not have to dust! The downside, of course, was that nothing within reach from the floor was safe from her scrutinizing examination or her razor sharp teeth. This may account for the fact that I spent an increasing number of hours out in the safety of the outdoors. This actually turned out better for me, because in the quiet of the land, one learns to think and create in a way that can only be experienced in nature.

1956

Sylvia, Queen of the House!

My relationship with Sylvia grew over time but not as I had expected. She developed into a pretty little girl who would never, as I had hoped, make a bush pal for me. Mother, on the other hand, got the daughter she wanted, albeit a bouncy little bundle of energy to try to teach. The two of them would spend many hours in the house and garden together, fulfilling a deep, mutual need. Everywhere Mother went, Sylvia went too, learning and absorbing her mother's vast resources of knowledge and skill.

A diet of garden dirt and cigarette butts

While she was still small, my sister developed the unimaginable habit of eating the crumpled remains of peoples' cigarettes. She was repeatedly scolded for this habit but continued despite the resistance. One day, my exasperated parents hauled her off to the town of Spirit River to see if the doctor could explain this strange behaviour. After careful examination, the doctor stated that their little girl was indeed quite healthy. Dr. Law stated that this nasty habit was simply caused by her body's need for whatever mineral it could extract from those old butts. I'm not sure that my confused mother ever did entirely buy that explanation, but we returned home, knowing that my sister was at least healthy. That must also have had an effect on my parents, though, because they both decided to quit smoking about that time. This promptly put an end to Sylvia's edible nicotine supply.

The last and strangest habit that my little sister developed was that of eating dirt. Not just any dirt, but the good, healthy, garden-variety dirt. Mother repeatedly scolded her, but in the end she gave in and the *Queen of the House* won again. When working in the garden, however, Mom was resigned to keep her little girl in a highchair nearby. This was a protective measure, I think, to ensure there would be enough soil left to replant the garden the following spring.

Every Christmas, we would decorate the living room in bright streamers and tinsel. Dad would sharpen the axe and ask me to go and help him get a Christmas tree. It was always a struggle to keep up to this giant as he strode through the deep snow on our way toward the forest. We would walk a long way, out along the fields and down over the banks of the creek where the great spruce trees grew. He would always coach me on how to choose the best tree, knock the blanket of snow off of it and with a mighty blow, chop it down. We duplicated that trip to the forest each year, which, over time, created many good memories of those special Christmas moments. Once the tree was trimmed and brought in to thaw out, we built a wooden stand for it or filled a lard pail full of dirt from the cellar to support it. Most years, we had to trim the tree down to size just to stand it up in the living room! Each Christmas, we looked forward to these sharp needled spruce trees that filled our home with such a delightful aroma.

Mother taught me the art of decorating the tree, which I still love to do and little sister Sylvia delighted in hiding under this annual decorative masterpiece. By the time Syl was a teenager, however, Mother had trained her in the fine art of decorating as well and Sylvia took over the job when I left home to explore the world.

A near drowning

Despite the brother-sister conflicts, I think we all benefited from the sheer entertainment value that my little sister gave us. I can recall our whole family picnicking upstream along the Burnt River not far from home. Mom had set out her usual Sunday afternoon culinary delights of potato salad and cold, fried chicken on a blanket by the water. Dad taught us kids to dog paddle across our favourite pool in the stream and we splashed and swam the afternoon away. This was a quiet and pretty hideaway with high riverbanks painted in the emerald green of seasonal berry bushes. Our little picnic spot was a favourite retreat for songbirds, and their joy was evident in the assortment of melody that echoed through the valley.

One warm Sunday, Dad had become momentarily distracted by something he was trying to teach me, when Mother yelled, "Frankie! Where is Sylvia?" Dad and I spun around to find that little sister was nowhere in sight. At first, we simply stood there, blinking dumbly in the afternoon sun. We were both half expecting this energetic little kid to pop up with a squeal and a splash, but the pond was quiet. The old inner tube remained floating mid stream, but still no sign of little sister. The water was still, as we stared in disbelief, trying to visualize where this little whirlwind might be hiding, when all at once I spotted one little leg clenched over the inner tube. "There she is!" I yelled. Dad dove for the centre of the pool, came up under the tube and flipped it over, revealing a frightened little half drowned girl. As he sat her up on the tube, the water virtually poured out of her eyes, ears and mouth! Father pushed the tube to shore and we *squeezed* the rest of the river out and laid her face down on the blanket to drain! Once she was dried out, that near death experience seemed to extract all of her energy. I don't recall that Sylvia was ever so brave in the water after that. She kept well away from the dugout at home and only played near shore when we went to the lake.

Where is Tarzan when you need him most?

I remember one day, when little sister had misbehaved, Mom was administering justice for the deed. I came upon the scene of her punishment and couldn't bear the sound of Sylvia's distress, so without careful selection of words, I told my mother off. This, of course, was a foolish thing to do because Mom would never stand being mean mouthed by the likes of me. To know my mother was to understand that she was lean, strong and fast, which meant that my clumsy, gangly frame had little chance of escape once she was provoked. The moment I realized my mistake, I ran, but ran in vain. (Try running in gum rubber boots!) Across the yard and out into the field I raced, but at each strained breath I could hear her pounding footsteps getting closer! Jumping over a board on the path, I shot a glance back to see if she was still gaining, only to find in horror that she had stopped to pick up the board and continued the chase. (Oh, where was Tarzan when I needed him most!) It was only a few futile moments then, before Mother Godzilla caught up and knocked my knees out from under me. Then I was sorry, oh yes I was, repentant even, but mad, real mad, and sore too, but after all I did deserve it! The only benefit gained from that chase was that the administration of Sylvia's punishment was cut short while Mother momentarily turned her attention to me.

My parents were never shy to correct what they saw going wrong in their children but at the same time they were quick to forgive and forget and get on with life. I appreciated the fact that although they had a keen sense of justice they also were never cruel or mean. Later in life, I began to realize that it would have been grossly unfair if they had let us continue to misbehave. Allowing us to think that we could be unfair, selfish, disrespectful, dishonest or unkind to people without certain reprisal would have set us children up for a dreadful awakening to reality as we grew older.

These were homemade lessons designed to prepare us for real life in the big world that as yet we knew nothing about. I am thankful for the strict upbringing that we received because it gave me an advantage over so many that had yet to learn those basic lessons of life. Sadly, newspaper court reports are full of accounts of people's mistakes that are clearly a result of the lack of discipline in their lives. I have seen so many people who have failed in almost every aspect of life because these simple, basic principles were lacking.

Obscene phone calls

My favourite little sister grew into a lovely young girl who could always be found at the centre of social activity in our town. I remember her as a tenderhearted girl who enjoyed the simple things of life and who was easily hurt by unkind words. The one

274

thing that my sister and I had in common was our appreciation for the uncomplicated company of the animal friends in our life. Our furry friends never held grudges, never said unkind words and were always quick to forgive our mistakes. Oh, if only our fellow humans were as wonderfully amiable as that. I am reminded of a quote that states, "Lord, please help me to be the kind of person that my dog thinks I am!"

Eventually, we grew out of our protective surroundings and were thrust unwillingly into the cruel and complicated world beyond our home. The next hard step in our social education would be that of "whom could we trust out there" and for my gentle little sister, this would be a challenge, difficult to master.

If pretty Sylvia had a natural gift, it was the ability to capture the attention of people around her, and from crib to basketball, she practiced her skill with conviction. Unfortunately, boys in particular have the distinction of being short-circuited by what they see, especially where pretty girls are concerned.

After our little socialite was in school for a few years, the telephone became her private office. As a result, an unfortunate problem developed. At that time, certain unintelligent callers became a veritable nuisance for Sylvia and the rest of our family with their obscene calls. These were boys of such simple minds that they were unable to engage in a fundamental conversation without sexual innuendos. Mindless boys like this are an unwanted plague of our society and a danger to the girls they stalk. Inevitably, these testosterone challenged males must face the truth, delivered either by their peers or by the law.

With my interest in electronics, I decided to invent a way to end this daily phone plague that we were experiencing. By rewiring my battery powered reel-to-reel tape recorder, I was able to record and play directly to the phone line. Calling the R.C.M. Police in Spirit River, I recorded their greeting and then saved it for the next time one of our dimwitted callers phoned. Sure enough, as soon as we knew it wasn't one of the neighbours calling, I pressed play on my tape recorder and the R.C.M.P. appeared to answer our phone. It wasn't long before the simpletons were discouraged with this confusing situation and quit calling.

The only people to suffer with this experiment were my dear mother and whomever she was calling to chat with. You see, for me to pull off such a feat, I had to practice, yes practice recording live voices to make sure my plan would work. My poor mother would be cheerfully talking to her friends and enjoying the conversation while I secretly tapped the phone line. I would then rewind my tape and in a break in the conversation, began playing their conversation back to them. These poor confused ladies tried repeatedly to answer the voice on the phone, until suddenly one would say, "Margie, where is your son?" Oops, time to disconnect and dash!

Sleight of hand

Serving remote farm communities with handy household products, in those days, were a couple of friendly, travelling salesmen. One gentleman in particular became very popular in our community because of his talents as a trickster and magician. The "Raleigh Man," as he was called, would make his rounds a couple of times a year, often arriving just in time for supper. Smart, real smart, I'd say. No one complained about his appetite because as you might expect, he would volunteer to perform for us after the meal was done. He knew the most unique and impossible card tricks that you could imagine, as well as a few sleight-of-hand tricks to top the evening.

With each visit, this friendly magician would have some new trick to dazzle us with so that we were never disappointed. Sister Sylvia would watch this man with awe as he performed each careful move and was fascinated with his talents. On one of his trips, however, when my big-eyed sister was standing intrigued with the performance, the Raleigh Man was testing our eye-hand coordination. He would hold up a two-dollar bill by one end and have us attempt to catch it between our fingers. He bravely announced that we could keep the two dollars if we could catch it. We carefully placed our fingers as close to the bill as possible, ready for the drop. Well, of course by the time we could see that he had let go, the bill had already passed through our fingers and we had missed it.

After we had all tried catching this elusive bill, my innocent little sister challenged him with this statement. "I could catch a twenty," she said, smiling. The man thought for a moment, glanced at my dad and winked, knowing that the twenty would be the same shape and weight and therefore just as difficult to catch as the two-dollar bill. Without hesitating, our magician friend unfolded a crisp twenty from his wallet and confidently held it up for little Syl to catch. He smiled as he said, "Go ahead, little girl." WAP! Crumple. That twenty-dollar bill promptly vaporized!

Sylvia stood there giggling, grasping his precious twenty dollars in her chubby little hand! I've never again seen such a shocked look on anybody's face as I did that summer evening. While my mother was sitting and laughing hysterically, the guy just stood there staring sadly at his empty hand. Sylvia ran off to plan her next shopping trip and I can't remember the Raleigh Man performing at our house again.

Attacked

On a busy Saturday, one summer, Mother sent her daughter over to the neighbour's house to borrow some baking supplies. Obediently, she rode off with her trusty bicycle in the afternoon breeze. As she neared the neighbour's house, she pedalled past their German shepherd dog outside who was wolfing down a bowl full of fresh, wild meat. The poor, unsuspecting kid never even saw the danger before it had knocked her off of the bike and onto the ground! That angry monster stood on her back and chewed her head and neck in a snarling frenzy while my sister screamed in terror. The neighbour lady finally came out and sent the dog running with the smack of a broom handle. Mother cleaned up my sobbing sister and Dad immediately rushed her off to the hospital for stitches. Her scalp and neck as well as her hands and arms were chewed up, not to mention the big puffy claw marks on her back.

That was the first of so many unfortunate dog *accidents* that I encountered in my lifetime that were the direct result of irresponsible dog ownership. Some dogs should be penned up, better trained or put down for safety sake, as accidents like this continue to occur all too often. People are often mutilated and sentenced to a lifetime of pain or disfigurement as a result. In this particular case, we learned that you should never, ever feed your dog a diet of raw, wild meat. The dog that attacked Sylvia was moved to the neighbours a mile away for safety sake, but I watched for months with my rifle handy for a chance to avenge my little sister. The question remains, do "all dogs" go to heaven? I don't think so!

Rescued from near death

Each quiet winter, Sylvia and I would enjoy bright days of sunshine, skating together on the dugout pond. We would shovel off a portion of the ice for free skating as well as clearing a great circle in the snow for games. Our snow circles had spokes that met in the centre so that we could play tag or a game called Fox and the Hound. Hollering and laughing until we were hoarse, we chased each other through the maze of ice trails, having great fun.

On days when we became bored, we might dress warmly and head out into the cold to go sliding. Syl and I would work together to carry water from the pond to "ice" our toboggan run out on the creek hill. For several years, we built runs so fast they would take your breath away.

Building snow tunnels were my specialty, and everyone enjoyed these frozen masterpieces, including little sister and the farm dogs. Snow caverns and tunnels formed an eerie, mystical world, lit by soft, diffused light. Once constructed, they could be used all winter and provided outdoor play spaces, sheltered from the wind. One particular snow cavern, which we had excavated, was on the exposed edge of a west-facing creek bank. The wind had hardened the snow into a drift that would easily hold our combined weight while standing on top. As the excavation grew bigger, I warned Sylvia that we should not venture up on top anymore because there was not much left underneath to support the roof. We played in that great snow castle, sometimes for whole days, building rooms and a living area under the snow.

One afternoon, while I was digging away on some new section of our snow cave, my sister forgot my warning and climbed up on the top of this giant drift. I hadn't noticed that she was gone until suddenly, the whole roof collapsed and our castle was crushed beneath the snowdrift above! I lay there, pinned by the weight of the roof, unable to move my body or to even call out. Panic gripped me as I struggled to move one limb at a time to free myself! My only thoughts were for air and to squirm out from under this dreadful weight.

Thankfully, under the snow there is a certain amount of air, and as I bashed away with my arms, I was able to get the snow away from my face to some extent. Little by little, I worked away for what seemed like a long time, breaking the heavy crust and pushing it down under my body. Then, I felt a tugging on my leg, and I could hear the frightened screams of my little sister as she pulled and dug around my legs. Within minutes, she had me out from under that massive drift and I was free! We just lay there in each other's arms, with streams of tears freezing to Sylvia's face as we rested in the quiet of the falling snow. Thank you, my little sister. Most kids would have panicked and ran off for home, which might have ended with my demise.

Deadly on the basketball floor

With five years' difference in our ages and of infinitely different interests, my sister and I grew further apart as the years went by. Syl had her friends and I had mine. She was interested in sports in school while the great outdoors were calling me. We seemed to only cross paths in the evening, when predictably, I would be coming home as she was going out.

Years went by, and after I had gone off to see the world, Sylvia became Father's "right hand man." She grew strong and helpful as a farm hand, slinging heavy hay bales and driving the tractor. I suppose this heavy exercise contributed to her reputation of being deadly on the basketball court. I believe I've heard that you dare not block her on the way to the hoop if you want to go home without bandages!

Sylvia eventually left the peace and quiet of our country home and ventured into the world. Her life then became so busy that I rarely heard how she was keeping or where she was living. Throughout the years, we were amused with the fact that when sister Sylvia did call, she almost always brought news of a newly arrived baby. In all, there were five such phone calls announcing five bouncy new arrivals. She is the mother of three strong and active boys and two beautiful girls.

Although Sylvia never became the *bush pal* I had originally hoped for, we have enjoyed our relationship as brother and sister. In recent years, we have spent many hours reminiscing the homestead years and looking through old photos. Sylvia is established with a good home, enjoys regular visits from her grandchildren and lavishes her fine cooking on all of her visitors.

Mother's indelible imprint

Mother passed away in 1982 due to complications resulting from emphysema. She had smoked for only twenty years out of her whole life, but this one mistake caused irreparable damage to her lungs, and sadly, death early in her life. It was a hard lesson learned from a hard world, but for Sylvia and I, it was an irreplaceable loss that we shall never get over. Gone were the wonderful mother, counsellor and willing listener that we both relied upon for so many years. Gone also was her constant love, understanding and stern direction for our lives. Thankfully, we retain awesome, vivid memories of a woman so outstanding that she is still a source of inspiration so many years later. When I listen to my sister speak of baking and cooking, or when recounting the wonderful farm years of growing up, I hear in her, our mother speaking.

Mother has left an indelible imprint of her character upon her children. May she ever enjoy her new, heavenly home.

Marjorie Greenfield
Our loving mother

Chapter
Twelve

Never reveal
your deepest secret

Charting the Hawaiian Islands

On a boring, early morning watch in the Operations Room of the St. Croix, I carefully coloured around the islands that were drawn on my plotting paper. The large 30 X 60 inch plot was a record of our ship's manoeuvres during our last deployment. The DDE (destroyer) was steaming north again after six weeks of training in the Hawaiian Islands and we were finally on our way home to Victoria. With the exercise over and the crew at rest, my mind drifted again to the bright skies and green fields of my childhood home, so far away. I realize that it won't seem to make sense that after enjoying six glorious weeks enjoying warm, turquoise waters, magnificent volcanic formations, jungles and palm trees, that I could even remember the far north. But yes, here I was, savouring the good memories of sailing under the glow of the Mauna Loa volcano, exploring the lava rock beaches of Hawaii and the jungles of Kawai and Molokai, but still with my heart and roots in northern Canada.

The Canadian government will never know how thankful I was for all the global exploration that they paid me to do. From the South Seas to the North Pacific, we flew our beautiful red and white flag that had become such a wonderful symbol of peace and hope to the world. Several times, I visited the cool waters of Alaska. Twenty five times, we sailed south to work with American forces out of San Diego, and throughout my career, my ship sailed to the Hawaiian Islands fifteen times. We explored every inlet and picturesque fjord along the British Columbia coast, while as part of Fourth Escort Squadron, we trained young Naval Officers in leadership and navigation. For me, the wonderfully quiet places away from civilization were the most beautiful. Even the open ocean reminded me of the wind blowing over a field of wheat with its rolling waves and prairie-like cloud formations.

R.C.N. Radar Plotter D.W. Greenfield

Top Secret

Finally, after almost eight exciting years aboard ship, I was transferred to a land assignment as a B Stand air controller at CanMarPacOps. Checking in for work at the Canadian Maritime Pacific Headquarters Operations building, through multiple levels of security, was a daily reality for the last couple of years of my Naval experience.

My Radar and Operations background were a prerequisite for those long months of working with international forces, intelligence briefings and tense, overseas phone calls I was about to experience. Assisting the Operations Officer, my desk held a phone that would connect me with any number of Air Force bases and government authorities at the touch of one single button. My counterpart in Halifax would call each shift to tell me what the weather was like in Nova Scotia (likely so I could feel sorry for him)! On the overhead speakers, the Vancouver International Airport flight control was broadcast day and night.

We often had an R.C.M.P. aircraft working in the area and Canadian or American Air Force on assignment out of McCord or Comox Air Force Bases. MarPacOps also monitored ship movement all over the Pacific; even down to the location of foreign fishing fleets operating near the British Columbia coast. The RCC (Rescue Coordination Centre), which was staffed twenty-four hours a day, also worked closely with our office to coordinate the various authorities needed for land and marine rescue. Consequently, our Operations Room at MarPac looked like something out of a James Bond movie, with floor to ceiling wall charts of various parts of the world and every imaginable mode of communication known to man. It was an immensely interesting place to work, albeit so very different from the ship-born Operations Room that I was accustomed to.

Cold war days

Those years were referred to as the "Cold War days" when tension with the former Soviet Union was high. The Soviets would periodically sneak across the *pond* (the Pacific) and test our defence shield, and we would in turn fly night flights over into Soviet waters. As a Radar Tech, I was asked to fly along on one lonely night patrol. We flew out of Comox Air Base with a long-range Canadair Argus and began a pre-arranged 12-hour patrol of launching and monitoring sonar buoys (undersea listening devices). The plane flew within sight of the Russian coastline and returned, carefully plotting every ship and submarine that we discovered along the way. The information was plotted, analyzed and shared with allied forces for military intelligence.

Here, I found myself in a secret world where I was not even allowed to discuss the details of my daily routine with my own wife. Daily intelligence briefings were most interesting as we monitored military movements around the globe. Each shift, working with international Armed Forces, R.C.M.P., Federal Fisheries and Coast Guard, was essential in keeping our coast and our country safe.

Wild roses and fresh cut hay

The Operations Room was a surreal world, far from the quiet forests and fields of the northland where I grew up. Going to work each day was then somewhat of a paradox for me because of the fact that, although I was here in Victoria working on my Naval career, I was also keenly aware that under the uniform, behind this secure perimeter, I was still a farm kid. Just beneath the crisply pressed tunic and official position, was the smell of fresh cut hay and wild, Alberta roses. This is one secret I was careful not to discuss in my surroundings. Another was the fact that although I had graduated from fleet school (a naval trades college), was proficient in anti-submarine warfare, navigation, radio, radar and electronics, seamanship, shipboard firefighting and naval operations, I kept hidden yet my deepest secret.

Never admit your deepest secret

Dyslexia (and likely a little attention deficit) had plagued me from my school days and continued to be problematic throughout my military and subsequent government careers. Learning to work alone, quickly and efficiently, became extremely vital so that my supervisors preferred not to team me up with someone else. When working closely with other people, I had little choice but to let them do all the thinking and planning while I passively agreed and did what they expected. A dyslexic mind works so differently from others that it's all but impossible to work closely together on any project where relative input is expected. Rarely was I embarrassed, though, and my secret was for the most part, kept hidden. When I found myself in the awkward face of being revealed, I was quick to make an escape, using any excuse to have time to work on the problem at hand on my own terms and on my own time. Short-term memory problems, inability to recall line data (numbered or lettered sequences, such as codes, etc.) or simply having to perform mathematical calculations in my head, were daily struggles that plagued me.

Escape to the wild lands

Most of my life I regarded myself as being dumb, as I had been rudely depicted on many occasion from toddler to adulthood. Thankfully, after nearly ten years, my move from the military to the Provincial Parks Service was a natural progression of events that led me back to more familiar surroundings. Working in the forest and wild lands of our great country, I had an advantage over many; I was at home once again in the quiet of the wilderness. Of course, as a Park Ranger, I always had an office to come back to, but for the most part I could escape to the quiet of the land and do my paper work or calculations where I had time and space to think.

I have written this account, not only for the historical and entertainment value, but also for those who may themselves have struggled with some degree of learning disability. I quickly learned that it was not wise to disclose the fact that I functioned differently than other people, but to simply take control of each task given to me and walk away with it so that I could work at my own speed. This was the only way to keep my Dyslexia a secret, although I constantly wished that I could improve my educational credentials.

Wanting a better education became a life long dream for me that would remain unrealized. To this day, I wish that I could have been an officer in the Navy rather than a tradesman. I would love to have gone beyond my private flight training to a commercial level or been able to obtain a degree so that I could have managed parks at a higher level. This, however, was not to be, and although I have a whole drawer full of certificates that attest to my striving for an education, there will never be a university degree framed on my wall.

That is, thankfully, one of the very few disappointments that I have had to endure. Being raised in those beautiful, peaceful surroundings of that humble homestead ushered in years of very positive and wonderful opportunities. I treasure albums full of grand adventures, an address book full of dear and interesting friends, wonderfully successful children, and sweet memories that could fill two life times.

Critical choices!

So, what did I learn as a Child of the Land that would be worth teaching to the most important people in my life such as my own grandchildren? I would want them to know that although we cannot choose our parents or the place of our birth, we will all get a chance to make our own choices as we grow older. Life is all about making choices. Whether we fail or succeed or are filled with joy or sadness, all has to do with the choices we will make as we travel through our life. Every decision we make is important, as many of our choices can and will lead to success or failure. I made many incorrect decisions that led to pain and sorrow, but what is the secret of success? Our daily journey involves risk, and we must calculate those risks to our advantage. Never, ever, blindly follow the crowd! It is far more important to pursue your personal interests and gifts than trying to be popular. I believe with all my heart that we have all been designed to excel in some special way.

Follow what is in your heart to do and not necessarily what your friends or your peers are doing. Without exception, we are all born of equal value, though not always with equal opportunity or with equal abilities.

I have concluded that we should never lose sight of the fact that each of us has some special gift within us. With this gift we can excel to improve the world around us and to help our fellow human beings. Our success and our dreams will be fulfilled in the pursuit of those gifts and talents. As for succeeding financially in this world, I believe that if you do what you love, (your personal gifts and talents) the money will follow.

This book has now come to an end, but my life has not. Each new day still holds more opportunity, with interesting people to meet and fun things to do. I received one of the greatest gifts ever just five years ago, when I asked my lovely Maggie for her hand in marriage. Now, I share my life with the most wonderful, intelligent and sensitive person I have ever encountered, and it only gets better. I look forward to exploring more of the world, enjoying our children and grandchildren and sharing the joy of our lives with everyone we meet. I have yet to climb all the mountains or to sail all the seas. There are lands to be explored and photographs to be taken. I have stories to write and poems to create and new people to know and love. I plan to wear out more pairs of hiking boots, more automobiles and enjoy many more banquets of delicious food. While there is air to breathe and the sun still shines in my heart, I want to encourage as many people as I can to make the most out of every minute of every day of the rest of their lives.

The End

Epilogue

Going home

Let your mind drift awhile and imagine that you are driving slowly through a picturesque countryside, following an old but familiar dirt road through the rich, green fields of what seems like paradise. Above, the sky is crystal blue and alive with a thousand migrant birds sharing their songs on gentle breezes. Fragrance fills the air with the delicate scent of sweet clover, wild roses and freshly cut hay.

The scene is quiet and peaceful as you roll slowly along, refreshed by the ambient beauty of the land. Sweet memories begin to flood into your consciousness as you stop along the roadway where long ago, an old farmstead once thrived. The remains of the buildings and fences are barely visible now in the deep, green grass and leafy poplar trees. Leaning on a weathered fence post, you linger and dream.

You can see, now overgrown with weeds and grass, where the farmyard and a busy driveway had once been, and an old, leaning electrical power pole still stands, its wires limp. Long gone are the friendly sounds of farm animals, replaced instead by wild creatures, nesting and playing in the country quietness.

There is a pretty, Redwing Blackbird singing from an old fence post nearby; and can you hear the killdeer calling in the lush pasture field beyond the house? The sun is hot, but the breeze helps cool your skin. You hear the sound of crickets, deep in the grass at your feet, and honeybees buzz around the roses along the old fence line.

296

Epilogue

As if standing at the very threshold of time, the scene before you stirs precious memories, long forgotten. Struggling with emotion, a tear finds its way down your cheek. Ever so faintly, you can smell the aroma of wood smoke and freshly baked bread as you close your eyes and reminisce, your thoughts far from the present.

Listen closely and allow your mind to travel back, say, forty years or more. Can you faintly hear the gentle mooing of cattle at the barn? Is that the sound of children's voices coming up the roadway with the merry chime of bicycle bells and laughter? A small dog is following, barking, chasing his tail.

Wait! Was that Mother calling? It must be near to suppertime...and is that Father you hear coming in from the field? Geese are honking and calling from the dugout pond and a wren is busily tending her nest in the twine box on the old binder. You take deep, nourishing breaths of rich, fresh air and cherish the fragrance of the wildflowers. A breeze tussles your hair and the slam of the old screen door jars you back to reality, to the present, with your heart still aching for the carefree days of youth.

But, those wonderful days are all gone, left somewhere in the dusty past of a busy life. Oh, that we could once more travel back to those trouble-free days, savour the sweet country air and hold Mother's hand as we walk in the garden.

Alas, the barn is now empty, the children have all grown and the old tractor is cruelly abandoned with willow trees growing through the wheels. The sadly leaning fence posts are all rotted and barely able to hold themselves up. An old swing seat sways gently in the breeze, hanging now by only one faded rope. You wipe away another stray tear and turn back to the road again. Sitting in the car with the door open and one foot out on that familiar clay road, your heart yearns for those wonderful days of old...carefree days of childhood when life was so very sweet. Closing the door now, you linger and savour one last time, the overgrown farmyard, the old weather-beaten buildings and those sweet memories that caress your consciousness.

Laboriously, your car rolls away as if straining to detach itself from the power of some mysterious magnetism from the past. Only a tuft of roadside weeds caught in your door is proof that you ever ventured far from the pavement. Picking up speed now, you reach to turn on your cell phone. Suddenly and gracefully, a white-tailed deer bounces across the road ahead of you, threatening to pull you back into the past. Struggling to remain in the present, you drive on, forcibly closing your storehouse of sweet memories and straining to contain the emotion blooming in your breast.

Something inside you cries out for a way to manipulate time, to go back, even for a day. Emotions still tingling, you concede to what you know is fact. Home and family, cherished the way you remember them have been hopelessly lost, far in the past.

Is this *all* there is? Could the scoffers be wrong after all? Is there a place beyond all dreams, beyond our wildest imagination, where a celestial home with timeless peace is awaiting us?

Epilogue

~~~~~~~~~~~~~~~~~~~~~~~~~~~~~~~~~~~~~

Yes, the old homestead continues to call, after all the years I have been away. I don't need much encouragement to drive out of my way to revisit that splendid, country beauty that can still be found in the Peace River area of Northern Alberta. Although the farm no longer looks like it did when I was a youth, it exudes a very real sense that this is still home. Often, when I tire of the daily struggle of life, my mind wanders back to those old creek banks where I can once again rest in the warmth of the bright, Alberta sun.

The Greenfield homestead showing the new house. 22 productive years of family business.

ISBN 142514810-7